Studies in Child Development

From Birth to Seven

STUDIES IN CHILD DEVELOPMENT

Titles in this series

NATIONAL CHILDREN'S BUREAU

From Birth to Seven

The Second Report of the
National Child Development Study
(1958 Cohort)

'Give me a child until he is seven and I will give you the man.'

Seventeenth-century Jesuit maxim

RONALD DAVIE
NEVILLE BUTLER
HARVEY GOLDSTEIN

with the assistance of
EVA ALBERMAN
EUAN ROSS
PETER WEDGE

LONGMAN
in association with
THE NATIONAL CHILDREN'S BUREAU

LONGMAN GROUP LIMITED
London

Associated companies, branches and representatives throughout
the world

© National Children's Bureau 1972

First published 1972
ISBN 0 582 32493 9

Printed in Great Britain by William Clowes & Sons, Limited,
London, Colchester and Beccles.

National Child Development Study
(1958 Cohort)

Sponsored and administered by:
National Children's Bureau

Co-sponsored by:
Institute of Child Health, University of London
National Birthday Trust Fund
National Foundation for Educational Research in England and Wales

In collaboration with:

England and Wales	{ Society of Education Officers { Society of Medical Officers of Health
Scotland	{ Association of Directors of Education { Association of School Medical and Dental Officers

CHAIRMAN OF CONSULTATIVE COMMITTEE:
Mary D. Sheridan, O.B.E., M.A., M.D., D.C.H.

CHAIRMAN OF STEERING COMMITTEE:
W. D. Wall, B.A., Ph.D.

EXECUTIVE CO-DIRECTORS:
Professor N. R. Butler, M.D., F.R.C.P., D.C.H.
Mrs M. L. Kellmer Pringle, B.A., Ph.D., Dip.Ed.Psych.

CO-DIRECTOR AND PRINCIPAL INVESTIGATOR:
R. Davie, B.A., Ph.D., Dip.Ed.Psych.

CO-DIRECTORS:
M. J. R. Healy, B.A.
J. M. Tanner, M.D., D.Sc., M.R.C.P.
W. D. Wall, B.A., Ph.D.

PRINCIPAL RESEARCH OFFICER:
P. J. Wedge, M.A., Cert.Soc.Sc., Cert.App.Soc.Stud.

STATISTICIAN:
H. Goldstein, B.Sc.

Contents

home; the relationship between overcrowding, lack of household amenities, educational attainment and social adjustment.

List of tables and figures

Acknowledgements

The National Child Development Study depends for its existence and continuance upon the support, co-operation and active help of a very large number of individuals and bodies. The sponsoring bodies of the study, the steering committee, the co-directors and the research team gratefully acknowledge this support and warmly thank all those who have been concerned.

In the first report of the study (Pringle, Butler and Davie, 1966) specific acknowledgement was made of the help of all those who had been involved up to that stage. However, tribute should be paid once more to the generous assistance of the Directors of Education, Principal School Medical Officers and of their staffs; and to the many individual head-teachers, teachers, medical officers and health visitors for the time and attention they gave to the study.

Special appreciation must also be expressed to the parents and the children in the study whose co-operation was so readily forthcoming.

Miss Ann Dufton together with some of her colleagues and students from Edge Hill College of Education carried out a small project to assess the reliability of the parental interview schedules; and this help, together with that of the schools and parents involved, is gratefully acknowledged.

Some of the staff who made substantial contributions at various times to the mounting of the study and the preparation of the data have now left the project. Special mention should be made of Dr M. Ball, Miss M. Levius, Mr C. Myler, Mrs J. Seglow, Miss V. Shenton, Miss S. Sherwin and Miss N. Thomas.

The preparation of the present book involved considerable technical, clerical and typing help, particularly at the drafting stages. Acknowledgements and thanks are due to other staff of the National Children's Bureau; Department of Growth and Development, the Institute of Child Health, University of London; Imperial College Computer Unit; University of London Computer Centre; and to members of staff and students of the Department of Child Health, University of Bristol. Particular mention should be made of Mr B. D. Adams, Mr A. F. Osborn, Miss J. Perrin, Miss J. Petzing, Mr A. Round, Mrs L. Thompson and Mr P. West.

The authors also wish to acknowledge and warmly thank the research team of the study and others for their very substantial contributions to the drafting of the book. Mr P. Wedge, with the assistance of Miss J. Petzing and the late Mr R. Hoyle, was responsible for the preliminary drafting of chapters 4 and 5 and Dr E. Ross for Chapters 6, 7, 9 and 14; Dr E. Alberman wrote Chapter 13 and helped in the final drafting of Chapters 7, 9, 14, 15 and 16. Dr Mary Sheridan did a great deal of work on the findings embodied in the section on hearing (p. 93). Dr M. L. Kellmer Pringle's guidance throughout and her helpful comments on drafts have been greatly appreciated, as have those of Mr Michael Healy.

The work reported was financially supported by the Department of Education and Science; the Home Office; the Scottish Education Department; and the Social Science Research Council.

Reference

PRINGLE, M. L. K., BUTLER, N. R. and DAVIE, R. (1966) *11,000 Seven-Year-Olds*, Longmans.

Foreword

Longitudinal studies of the development of large groups of children demand unusual determination, patience and courage. The work produces no quick rewards: the way ahead is long and at times laborious; and there will often be onlookers ready to criticise specific aspects from the standpoint of their own particular discipline.

However, no-one can cavil here at the rich harvest of facts described and discussed; nor at the fascinating, often challenging, insights into the interplay of health, education and home environment with children's development. '11,000 Seven-Year-Olds' (Pringle, Butler and Davie, 1966) gave us more than a glimpse of the potential of the National Child Development Study (1958 Cohort). 'From Birth to Seven' reinforces this impression.

One of the most impressive features of the study is the success with which the children were traced, six years after their birth. To gather information on 92 per cent of a sample as large as this, demands not only very efficient administration but a high level of diplomatic skill. Furthermore, the fact that every local education authority in England, Scotland and Wales was a willing collaborator and only 84 parents out of more than 16,000 refused to take part reflects a strong tradition of voluntary co-operation in this kind of study of which Britain can justifiably be proud. This very high return has strengthened the study by ensuring the representative nature of the sample.

The presentation of the results of the study posed a difficult dilemma for the research team. The detailed analyses were clearly going to be of great value to administrators and policy makers as well as to research workers. However, there was a much wider audience that the research team were anxious to reach: ordinary teachers, doctors, social workers, psychologists and others in their schools, clinics and hospitals. This latter group by and large is interested less in the detail than in an account of the major findings presented in a readable, non-technical form, and at a reasonable cost. It was clear that both objectives could not be achieved in a single volume. The solution achieved can be commended to other research workers faced with the same dilemma. The main results have been presented and discussed in one volume with the practitioner very much in mind; no statistical knowledge is assumed and a minimum of technical terms are used. A second volume with the same text but including a very detailed statistical appendix and photostats of the questionnaires used has been produced for those whose work demands this.

It would be superfluous here to add to the many conclusions which the authors discuss. But readers of these conclusions should bear in mind the political and social context of this discussion. First the policy. Scholars and scientists will continue to argue—and fruitfully—about the explanation of children's development and attainments, their health and social adjustment, and about the causal influences exerted by their genetic endowments, their parents, teachers, peer groups, living conditions and other factors. But for administrators and policy makers one thing is now beyond argument. Whatever the reasons for poor attainment or poor health, it is the community's responsibility to find ways of improving it. It used to be assumed that the community's responsibility had been fulfilled once the resources for education or community health had been provided; from that point it was the responsibility of children and parents to seize their opportunities. Educational progress and equality of educational opportunity were measured by the inputs of staff, buildings and expenditure. Now we ask about the *outputs*. How much do children learn? How far behind the others do the weaker performers fall? What is the 'take up' of health and social services? What can we do to improve the situation?

The patterns glimpsed in the National Child Development Study are so deeply embedded in this country's economic and social structure that they cannot be greatly changed by anything short of equally far-reaching changes in that structure. Living conditions for families with young children probably vary more greatly—inequalities are sharper—than for any other type of household. Many children live in the newest and leafiest suburbs within easy reach of well paid jobs in expanding industries, new schools and shops, extensive parks and all the advantages of urban and rural life. But many others live in overcrowded quarters where people are constantly on the move, social organisation is weak, unemployment is rife, schools are old and under-staffed, and there is no open space or legitimate playground.

Such patterns are the outcome of a long history of economic and social development, reinforced or modified by the policies followed by central and local authorities for family allowances, employment, housing, transport and land uses. Too often they are re-emphasised rather than corrected by the deployment of educational resources. There is no time to be lost in setting about the task of changing them.

DAVID DONNISON
Director, Centre for Environmental Studies

References

PRINGLE, M. L. KELLMER, BUTLER, N. R. and DAVIE, R. (1966). *11,000 Seven-Year-Olds*, Longmans.

1. The plan of the book

What kind of reader?

This book is written for all whose professional work is concerned with children and also for the interested parent. It is essentially a description of the abilities and attainments, behaviour, physical development, health, home environment and birth history of a large and representative group of seven-year-old children in England, Scotland and Wales. The children, nearly 16,000 in all, were born in one week of March 1958.

The detailed results are so extensive that to have tried to present and discuss them all in one book would have made it unwieldy, not to mention expensive. Furthermore, at any one point, the presentation would have been too detailed for most readers.

It was decided therefore to place the tables of results, most of the detailed descriptions of the sample, the reliability figures, etc. in a statistical appendix which is included in the hardback edition of the book but not in the paperback version.

The book itself is written in non-technical language and assumes no specialist knowledge on the part of the reader. A few tables will be found, where this type of presentation is felt to be useful, but they are simple in form, and the results are percentaged to the nearest whole number. However, diagrams are often preferred. Results in the text, too, are usually given in percentage form. No attempt is made to be exhaustive where an example will suffice to illustrate the salient point.

In short the book is not written for the research worker so much as for the 'practitioner' and the administrator who are concerned with children's development in its many aspects, and in the effects of policy and practice upon children's lives. Nevertheless, it is hoped that research workers will find much to interest them, and that the appendix, in particular, will prove a valuable storehouse of information.

The logic and planning of the book implied that any description of the use of statistical techniques would be an encumbrance. Such techniques after all are a means to an end; and it is only the end which is of interest to the majority of readers. They are often not in a position to judge whether or not the statistical methods used are appropriate and so *de facto* have no choice but to trust the author's judgment. On the other hand, the details of analyses must be recorded somewhere so that anyone who is interested in this aspect may have access to them.

Therefore it was decided to make no mention of statistical techniques in the text, nor to levels of significance and so on. All these details will be found in the appendix. It may be assumed that when differences between groups are mentioned in the text, these have been tested, where appropriate.

The use of 'social class'

'Social class' is a term and a concept which will be encountered frequently in the pages which follow. What is meant by the term? And how and why have we used it?

In everyday language 'class' is often used as an evocative term with undertones of social prejudice. Expressions such as 'middle class' or 'working class' frequently imply a value judgment; and this judgment will be influenced by one's view of society or one's political standpoint. Occasionally, these values are explicit as in the terms the '*upper* classes' or the '*lower* classes'. Many people in our society—some much more intensely than others—think socially in terms of 'them' and 'us'; and 'class' is often a part of this thinking.

In this general context, 'class' carries some implication of a person's standing—or even his 'worth'—within a hierarchical society. It is this element which adds the emotive flavour.

The term is not used in this rather subjective sense here; certainly there is no suggestion that any assessment of the parent's 'worth' is being—or could be—attempted. In the pages which follow, 'social class' is used exclusively to describe the occupational group of the children's fathers. Inevitably, any such grouping will be hierarchical in so far as it relates to the level of skill (or training) required.

In Britain the most frequently used classification of occupations is that adopted by the Registrar General for census purposes (H.M.S.O., 1960). This is modified in detail from time to time but the general outline remains. The basic framework is of five occupational groups which are termed Social Classes I to V. Social Class I consists of occupations which require the highest professional qualifications, usually a university degree or its equivalent. Occupations in Social Class II also often demand a professional qualification and, for example, school teachers and many higher civil servants are in this group; it also includes managers and others of a similar position in industry or commerce even if they are 'unqualified'. Virtually all the occupations in these two groups are of a non-manual nature.

Social Class III, by far the largest single group, is usually subdivided into a non-manual and a manual section. In the former, are placed almost all the remaining non-manual occupations, such as foremen in industry, shop assistants and clerical workers. The occupations in the other section are all regarded as 'skilled manual'. Social Class IV consists almost exclusively of semiskilled manual occupations and Social Class V contains the unskilled manual occupations.

The classification is summarised in Table 1 together with the proportions of children in the study whose fathers fell into each group. In a little under 3 per cent of the households there was no father or male head.

Table 1. Classification of occupations (N = 14,495)

Social Class		%
I	Higher professional	5
II	Other professional and technical	14
III (non-manual)	Other non-manual occupations	10
III (manual)	Skilled manual	44
IV	Semi-skilled manual	17
V	Unskilled manual	6
No male head of household		3

With very few exceptions, the first three groups in Table 1 contain non-manual or 'white-collar' jobs and these groups will be described as 'middle class'. The occupations in the next three groups are almost exclusively of a manual nature and these will be referred to as 'working class'. The individual groups will be described as in the table (Social Class I, etc.).

Why is a classification of occupations of value in studying children? In our society a man's occupation tends to be related to the way he lives outside his work situation. At the most obvious level it will be linked to his income and hence to the kind of house he can afford and often to the kind of neighbourhood in which he chooses—or has—to live. The classification of occupations is directly related to qualifications, training and skill; and therefore it is often linked to the level of education. A less direct but still quite marked association can be shown between social class—as we shall now term it—and attitudes, most obviously to education, but also to child rearing. The middle-class family is more likely to take a keen interest in the children's formal education and have higher vocational aspirations for them than the working class family.

In short, social class is a convenient and useful indirect measure of many aspects of children's environment which will to some extent shape the way they develop. As might be expected, social class differences are usually most evident when the focus of interest is on educational progress, behaviour, interests and attitudes. But they can also be seen when physical attributes are studied: children of middle-class parents are in general taller and heavier than those of working-class parents. Even mortality and morbidity figures show similar trends. It is disturbing to note, for example, that although infant mortality has declined markedly in Britain over the past fifty years, the relative positions of the social class groups has remained the same.

Social class does not merely reflect environmental influences; there are hereditary factors too. The precise contribution of 'nature' and 'nurture' is still fiercely debated in some circles but this need not concern us here. It is extremely unlikely that all children are conceived, let alone born, with an *equal* potential for physical growth and intellectual development. The fact that children of professional workers are taller and more intelligent than children of unskilled manual workers is in some measure due to heredity. However, the contribution played by the environment in the development of stature will almost certainly be less than in the development of intelligence.

It should be stressed that social class is only of relevance in looking at group differences. An individual working-class child may very well be taller and more intelligent than an individual middle-class child, or even than most middle-class children. What then is the value of examining social class trends?

If it can be shown that certain aspects of children's development or function are *not* related to social class, the search for explanation or causes can be directed elsewhere. By the same token, the demonstration of a relationship between social class and a facet of development or function will prompt a narrowing of the search for causal factors and may have important implications for policy or practice. Preventive measures in the fields of child health, education or social work depend upon the ability to identify vulnerable children at an early stage. Where preventive measures are in operation, as, for example, with infant welfare clinics, it can be shown (see Chapter 6) that certain social class groups are much less likely to use them than others. This may—indeed should—prompt some reappraisal of the existing system.

However, the identification of social class differences should be seen as the first step towards a deeper more probing analysis. In our study some of these further analyses have been done, some remain to be done and others need the kind of additional investigation which only a smaller-scale more intensive study can carry out.

Social class reflects a large number of potentially important circumstances and it can be used as a base from which to conduct further analyses. To take an example, it is known that middle-class children have higher educational attainments than working-class children. It is also known that middle-class parents tend to show more interest in their children's progress at school than do working-class parents. Finally, it can be shown that children whose parents are interested do better at school than other children. The question which immediately occurs is: do the children of interested parents perform better at school (in general) than other children because they are more often middle-class children (with all that this implies) rather than because of their parent's interest?

One way of tackling this question would be to look at each social class group separately and see whether *within each group* the children of interested parents do better. This analysis was in fact carried out for the first report (see p. 25) and is essentially the kind of analysis which is often reported in the present book.

Of course, there are likely to be other relevant factors which are operating within each social class group and these may be clouding the issue. For example, family size may be linked to both parental interest and educational attainment. Where appropriate, allowance is also made in the analysis for such factors.

In short, social class is a useful measure for exploring the effects upon children's development of a wide range of circumstances. Furthermore, the identification of a social class difference may in itself indicate a need to re-examine policy or practice.

Mention should be made of the use of the word 'effect' in relation to the analyses described in the book. In normal usage, the word implies some causal connection between two events or circumstances; indeed, it is often used in this sense in the chapters which follow, when the *possible* implications of various circumstances for children's subsequent development are discussed in general terms. However, it is also sometimes used in discussing the actual analyses which have been carried out; and in these cases there is no implication that the relationships involved are necessarily of a direct cause–effect nature. It is used rather as a kind of 'verbal shorthand', which avoids clumsy and often complex sentence construction.

For example, 'the effect of social class on reading attainment' implies that there is a relationship between social class and reading attainment but not that the link is a causal one. Similarly, in Chapter 4 an investigation is carried out of the 'effects of family size upon reading and arithmetic attainment and social adjustment in school after allowance has been made for the effects of social class and country'. It will be clear from the discussion of the results of this analysis that although an attempt has been made to separate out the overlapping relationships involved, no conclusions can be reached that the size of the family in itself *causes* poor attainment.

Regional variations

One of the possibilities which a *national* study of children's development offers is that of making regional comparisons. They are of interest and value principally because they prompt questions about the reasons for any marked variations within Britain. The answers to these questions may throw light upon, for example, parental attitudes, differences in child rearing practice, differences in educational methods and in child health. In addition, they may point to gaps and inequalities in services provided for children (Taylor and Ayres, 1969).

The term 'region' may mean one thing to a geographer and another to an administrator. For some purposes the boundaries of regions may be loosely defined whilst for others an exact definition is needed.

The Registrar General's regional statistics for England are based on precisely defined 'standard' regions. The regional boundaries were changed in 1965 to bring them in line with the regions used for economic planning leaving one fewer in number. However, the material for the study was gathered in 1965 and so the old standard regions are used to present results. These regions are as follows: Northern, North Western, East and West Ridings (of Yorkshire), North Midland, Midland, East, London and South Eastern, Southern, South Western. In addition results are given separately for Wales and Scotland. For some analyses the first five regions mentioned above are grouped together to give a 'northern zone' of England and the remainder make up a 'southern zone'.

The numbers of children in the study in the regions and in Scotland and Wales are shown in Table 2 and the percentages are shown in Fig. 1. Regional results are only mentioned in the text where they are felt to be of particular interest or value. A detailed breakdown of results by region is given in the Appendix.

In considering any regional differences shown in the study two points should be borne in mind. First, our sample is a sample of children and not of, say, families or schools or local authorities. For example, the results on p. 51 describe the proportions of seven-year-old *children* living

Figure 1. Proportion of study children by region and country

Table 2. Number of study children by region and country

North Western	1991
Northern	1129
East and West Ridings of Yorkshire	1287
North Midland	1185
Eastern	1182
London and South Eastern	2826
Southern	953
South Western	932
Midland	1510
Wales	825
Scotland	1648
Total	15468

in overcrowded conditions in various regions and not the proportion of overcrowded *families*. These other results (i.e. for families) would be related to the figures we produce but they would not be the same.

The second fact to be borne in mind is that the regions vary in their social class distribution and there is a great deal of evidence presented later to show that social class is closely related to many aspects of children's development. Some regional differences are mere reflections of this social class variation, whilst others are not. Time has not always permitted the more detailed analyses required to determine whether particular regional variations can be explained in terms of social class. References are made in the text where this is relevant. Figure 2 shows

Figure 2. Percentage of middle class study children by region and country

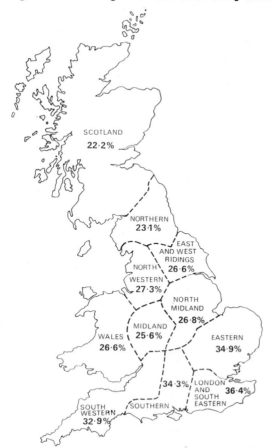

the proportion of children from middle-class families in the nine regions of England and in Scotland and Wales.

References

REGISTRAR GENERAL (1960) *Classification of Occupations*, H.M.S.O.

TAYLOR, G. and AYRES, N. (1969) *Born and Bred Unequal*, Longman.

2. Background to the study

The 1958 Perinatal Mortality Survey

In 1958 information was gathered on virtually every baby born in England, Scotland and Wales during the week 3 to 9 March. This survey (Butler and Bonham, 1963; Butler and Alberman, 1969) sponsored by the National Birthday Trust Fund, was designed to study the administration of British maternity services and investigate the causes of perinatal death (stillbirths and deaths in the first week).

The results of the survey highlighted sharply the increased perinatal mortality risk which is associated with certain clearly identified antenatal, social and obstetric conditions. For example, the risk of a perinatal death where a mother was having her fifth or subsequent baby was 50 per cent greater than average. Similarly, increased risk was associated with unskilled occupational status (30 per cent greater than average); maternal age over 40 (100 per cent greater); severe toxaemia in the mother (over 150 per cent greater); and heavy smoking during pregnancy (over 30 per cent greater). The identification in the survey and elsewhere of these and other high risk groups has made possible more concentration of medical resources upon mothers in most need.

This 'cohort' of children, numbering some 17,000 at birth, was unique for a number of reasons: it was a representative national group, selected only by date of birth; the very high proportion of returns (an estimated 98 per cent of all babies born in the week) virtually eliminated the possibility of bias; and the comprehensive nature of the perinatal data was unparalleled in the world for any national cohort.

The National Child Development Study (1958 Cohort)

In 1964 the opportunity arose to trace and study these children again and the National Child Development Study (1958 Cohort) was set up for this purpose. It is the results of this first follow-up, when the children were seven years old, which are presented and discussed here. At the time of writing information from a second follow-up when the children were eleven years old is being checked and prepared for analysis. It is hoped that it will be possible to continue to study the children throughout their childhood and into adult life.

Aims and scope of the study

Perhaps the most obvious value of the study lies in the *descriptive* material it yields. Surprisingly little objective information is available about normal children; and what information there is needs constantly bringing up to date in these times of rapid change. This kind of material is the backcloth against which the teacher, doctor or psychologist can see the individual child. It should also enable the administrator and the policy maker to monitor the effects of existing policy and practice and highlight any need for change. Many parents too can be reassured by a knowledge that what otherwise might be seen as a matter for concern is in fact quite common amongst children. We are looking, then, at a representative *cross-section* of children at certain ages in order to describe their behaviour, their health, their physical development, their educational standards and their home environment.

But if this were the only aim, it would be more convenient—and, incidentally, cheaper—to look at different groups of children of different ages. Why, then, do we take the trouble and go to the expense of tracing and following up the same group of children over a considerable period? This 'longitudinal' approach is valuable because certain kinds of question can be answered satisfactorily only in this way. At the descriptive level it is important to know, for example, not just how many children are backward readers at seven and at eleven years of age but whether they are the same children at eleven as at seven. This may have implications, say, for the provision of remedial education.

However, many of the questions for which we most want to find answers go beyond mere descriptions. And many of them begin with the word 'why'. Why do some children become backward readers? Why are some children maladjusted? What are the results of a broken home? Are certain kinds of birth complications related to subsequent disability?

Unfortunately, definitive answers to these kinds of questions are extremely difficult to pin down. The most obvious reason for this is that we cannot experimentally expose children to potentially adverse circumstances in order to measure the effects. And where the adverse circumstances occur spontaneously, we cannot know whether it is these *per se* or their precursors which lead to the observed results.

There are therefore two approaches which offer some chance of throwing light on these problems. First, the previous history of children already known to be handicapped in some way can be examined. The principal difficulty here is that records are rarely complete and people's memories are at best fallible and at worst influenced by their knowledge of subsequent events. The second approach is to follow the progress of a group of children who are known to have been in adverse circumstances. In order to attempt to isolate the effects of these circumstances it is usually necessary also to follow up a control group of children who are 'matched' with the others in every important respect except the particular circumstances which are being investigated. But it is impossible to match two groups of children in every respect and it is not always possible to know for certain and in advance what are the important factors.

The large-scale, longitudinal study offers solutions to some of these problems. For example, there is no necessity to make a decision at the outset as to what factors to match for, if one is interested in the progress of a particular group of children. Secondly, one can look back at the previous history of children who are doing badly, or well, in the knowledge that the records are complete and that the information is not influenced by the memory of subsequent events.

Furthermore, having isolated some aspect of the children's earlier life which appears to be related to their subsequent development, it is then possible to look at the subsequent development of all the children with similar histories. For example, suppose it is found that delinquents tend to come from broken homes. This would be interesting, although not novel. But it is a fact of everyday experience that not *all* children from broken homes become delinquent. A longitudinal study makes it possible to say what proportion of children from broken homes become delinquent, i.e. what is the risk involved. It also holds out the possibility of identifying some of the circumstances which may counteract a potentially damaging experience. In terms of future preventive action, the white sheep are at least as important to study as the black sheep.

The longitudinal aspects which can be examined in the study so far, relate to the associations between circumstances surrounding the birth and the children's development at the age of seven. But the associations between, say, different aspects of the children's environment and their development at the age of seven are also of interest. For example, in Chapter 5 the relationship between poor amenities in the home and children's educational performance is examined. In Chapter 10 we look at the relationship between social adjustment and reading attainment.

In short, the value of the study lies principally in its longitudinal character. However, each follow-up yields valuable descriptive material about a representative group of British children and also permits interesting and important relationships to be studied at one point in time.

The aims also include a study of the services provided for children. Each follow-up produces descriptive information, for example, about the proportion of children who are receiving special help in school; who have been to a health or dental clinic; or who are receiving speech therapy. Furthermore, it is of considerable value to know something about the kinds of families who use these facilities. To what extent do the families most in need utilise such services? In a longitudinal context, an evaluation of the results of the use of different services becomes possible.

Of course, this kind of study has its limitations. For example, the information which it is practicable to gather on 16,000 or so children circumscribes the kinds of question which can be answered. It may not be detailed enough; or some verification may be needed of particular items. For these reasons special studies, not reported here, have been carried out on certain groups of children from within the main cohort. In a study of those children with physical or sensory handicaps, for example, hospitals were contacted for confirmation of medical histories. In a study of the children who had been 'in care' during their first seven years, supplementary information was gathered from local authority children's departments. The adopted children were the subject of another study, in which the adoptive parents were interviewed by a research officer. The most detailed special study so far has been of the 'gifted' children in the cohort, who have all been interviewed by a psychologist and their parents interviewed by another research officer.

In these two last mentioned projects, it has been possible to gather the quality of information which only a small-scale study can yield. At the same time the children can be seen against the backcloth of the large representative cohort. The two kinds of study are therefore complementary and derive strength from each other.

Gathering the information

The information on the children in the first follow-up was gathered from three main sources: from schools by means of a schedule completed by the head-teachers and class-teachers (the *Educational Assessment* booklet), a few specific tests and other assessments; from mothers and sometimes fathers, who were interviewed by an officer of the local authority, usually a health visitor, using a structured interview schedule; and from school health services, who undertook medical examinations, carried out some special tests and completed a medical schedule.

In selecting the tests to be used and designing the schedules, there were two major considerations. First, the total amount of information which it was practicable to collect and analyse was an important issue. The teachers, health visitors, doctors, parents and children were giving voluntarily of their time and reasonable bounds were essential, not only to gain co-operation in the first follow-up but also to ensure that support in future follow-ups was not being mortgaged. From a research viewpoint, the number of separate items of data already available from the perinatal survey was close to two million. Modern computing processes can handle a large volume of data but all information has to be scrupulously checked; and there were real dangers that the project might become overburdened by the data processing aspects if fairly stringent limits were not set.

Secondly, the kind of information to be gathered had carefully to be considered. Many different observers and reporters were to be involved and it was vital that any information they gave should be comparable. This meant making the questions as objective as possible and ensuring that they were free of any ambiguities. From the standpoint of the analysis to follow it was essential to have information which ultimately could be recorded as a series of impulses on magnetic tape for computer analysis.

This requirement need not be as inhibiting as it may appear and, if nothing else, it forces the research worker to think very carefully about each question and to anticipate possible replies. For example, it was important to ascertain whether, and if so to what extent, the parents were interested in their children's education; and the children's teachers were the most obvious and appropriate source of information. Since it is possible that there would be a different answer in respect of a mother and a father, two questions were necessary. The questions would in essence be subjective because the teachers would be drawing inferences from a variety of 'clues'. Perhaps the most reliable clue would be whether the parents had visited the school and enquired about their child's progress. But the teachers might also infer the level of interest from chance remarks made by the children and this would be less reliable. The teachers might even be influenced—perhaps unconsciously—by irrelevant clues such as the children's speech or dress.

The ideal question, of course, would be one which requires no inferences but nevertheless provides the necessary information. With this in mind, the teachers were asked to say whether or not the parents had discussed their children with them during the current school year. The answers could thus be reduced to a simple Yes or No. However, it is possible that some parents who were interested were prevented by other commitments from visiting the school. For this reason, the teachers were also asked whether the parents showed interest in their children's education. In order that the answers could be analysed and compared, the teachers were presented with a number of possible replies: over-concerned and/or setting too high a standard; very interested; shows some interest; shows little or no interest; can't say or inapplicable. One of the difficulties in framing these possible replies is to ensure that there is a sufficient number to cover most if not all contingencies but not so many that the teachers would find it difficult to make a judgment as to the right one.

Of course, some questions are more straightforward than this but it illustrates well the problems which arise. A good questionnaire might be likened to some works of art in that the apparent simplicity of the finished product is only reached after a multitude of abortive attempts and a great deal of soul-searching!

The material for the study was tried out in a number of local authorities before it was finalised. The schedules which were finally used are reproduced in full in the Appendix, as are those tests which are not available in published form. All of the material was despatched in bulk to local authority health and education departments. The departments arranged for its completion and its eventual return to the research team.

The educational assessment

First, certain basic facts had to be established about the children's school environment, such as the type and size of school and the size of class. Some information was obtained, too, about less tangible aspects such as the contact between the school and the home and the basis on which children were allocated to classes. Finally, a fairly comprehensive picture was needed of the individual child: his abilities, his behaviour and adjustment and the interest shown by parents. Six different forms of assessment were decided upon:

1. The *Educational Assessment* booklet which asked for information about the school and its organisation, the relationship between the school and the parents, and which required assessments by the teacher of the child's abilities and attainments and certain aspects of his behaviour, notably his physical co-ordination and speech.
2. The *Bristol Social-Adjustment Guide* (Stott, 1963) to obtain a picture of the children's behaviour in the school setting. The *Guide* is a four-page booklet containing some 250 descriptions of behaviour. The teacher is asked to underline the descriptions which best fit the child. Items of

behaviour which are, in varying degrees, deviant or which may be symptomatic of emotional disturbance or social maladjustment are later identified by means of a system of coding. It is thus possible by summing the number of coded items to derive a quantitative assessment of the child's adjustment in school: the higher the score, the more indications there are of deviant behaviour.

3. The *Southgate reading test* (Southgate, 1962) for an objective assessment of the children's reading ability. This test essentially assesses word recognition. The children are asked to select from a number of words the one which corresponds to a picture in the test booklet; in other items the teacher reads out a word and, again, the children are asked to identify the word from those which they have before them.

4. The *'copying designs' test* to obtain some assessment of the children's perceptual-motor ability. Six designs were presented: a circle, square, triangle, diamond, cross and star. The children were asked to copy each design twice.

5. The *'drawing a man' test* as an indication of the children's general mental and perceptual development as well as other maturational aspects. The marking of this test was completed too late to include the results, which will be reported elsewhere.

6. The *'problem arithmetic' test* to assess the children's ability in this field. There were ten problems graded in level of difficulty. In order to avoid penalising the poor readers, the teachers were asked to read the problems to the children if necessary.

The parental interview

A schedule had to be designed which would be suitable for completion by a health visitor on interviewing the child's mother. It was felt that basic contemporary information about the child's development and environment should have first priority since in general this would be more reliable (i.e. less subject to any bias or simple inaccuracy of memory) than retrospective details. Reliability was also important in determining what retrospective information to collect. For example, the precise ages at which certain developmental milestones (e.g. sitting, standing, walking, talking) were attained would have been valuable to know but it was felt that at best the mother's memory might be faulty, particularly if she had a large family. At worst, her memory in this and other respects could be influenced by the child's subsequent development. In consequence, the questions on milestones were confined to asking, for example, whether or not the child was walking by eighteen months or talking (i.e. joining two words) by the age of two.

The information sought about the family and the home included the size of the family (adults and children); the parental situation (i.e. natural parents, adoptive, etc.); the father's occupation and education; the mother's work, if any; the type of accommodation, the tenure and the number of rooms; and household facilities (garden, yard, bathroom, etc.)

Retrospective information about the child included separations from the mother; pre-school experience (nursery schooling, playgroup attendance etc.); any periods 'in care'; attendance at infant welfare clinics; hospital admissions and specialist clinic attendances; and other details of medical history.

Current information was sought about many aspects of the child's behaviour; his physical co-ordination; and his adjustment at school.

The medical examination

A comprehensive medical examination of each child was felt to be an essential part of the follow-up not only to identify those children with handicapping conditions but also to spot relatively minor defects, which may nevertheless be associated with underfunctioning or educational difficulties.

It was important in this examination, as for other aspects of the study, to standardise the procedure as far as possible in order to obtain uniform criteria for clinical observation. Thus, the doctors were not asked merely to examine each child's ears and comment on any abnormalities noted. Instead, specific questions were asked about, for example, any signs of past or present otitis media, obscuring of the drum and deformity of the external ear. Where abnormalities or any dysfunction were noted, the doctors were asked for written amplification. The questions were set out systemically (central nervous system, cardio-vascular system, etc.).

In the case of tests of function and examination of the special senses, the conditions for the examination were given in detail in order to ensure that the results would be as comparable as possible.

The examination included measurements of height, weight and head circumference; tests and clinical assessments of vision, speech and hearing, including an audiogram; a urine test; assessments of motor co-ordination and laterality; and a full clinical examination.

References

BUTLER, N. R. and BONHAM, D. G. (1963) *Perinatal Mortality*, Livingstone.

BUTLER, N. R. and ALBERMAN, E., eds (1969) *Perinatal Problems,* Livingstone.

STOTT, D. H. (1963) *The Social-adjustment of Children: Manual to the Bristol Social-Adjustment Guides,* University of London Press.

SOUTHGATE, V. (1962) *Southgate Group Reading Tests: Manual of Instructions,* University of London Press.

3. The first report

In 1966 a report on the first follow-up of the children was prepared for the Plowden Committee.* However, since this had to be completed only eighteen months from the commencement of the study its findings were of an interim nature. It was concerned for the most part with the children in England and the results were produced before a small residue of 'late returns' could be included. This report was published in part as Appendix 10 (Volume 2) of the Plowden Committee's report and also separately (Pringle, Butler and Davie, 1966). All the major conclusions reached remain unchanged in the light of the full analysis now completed and are also unaltered by the addition of the results for the Scottish and Welsh children.

For those readers familiar with this first report, it would be tedious to go over old ground. However, since many of the results presented here assume a knowledge of the earlier findings, it would perhaps be confusing to some readers if these findings were not mentioned. Therefore, results from the first report are presented in summary form:

Educational factors

Reading ability

Three criteria were used in assessing the children's reading ability: performance on a standardised test of word recognition (the Southgate reading test); the stage reached by the child in the school's reading scheme; and the teacher's rating of reading ability on a five-point scale.

Judged by all three criteria, girls were found to be better readers than boys. A comparison was also made between our results and a study conducted in 1954 (Morris, 1959). The conclusion was reached that in

* The Central Advisory Council for Education (England) which under the chairmanship of Lady Plowden considered 'primary education in all its aspects and the transfer to secondary education'. Their report, *Children and their Primary Schools*, was published in 1967 by H.M.S.O.

the country as a whole, the number of poor and non-readers trans-
ferring to junior schools and classes had dropped considerably in the
interval from 1954 to 1965.

A little under half of the children—in the final stages of their infant
schooling—had not reached a stage of reading where they could make
optimal progress without further specific help in the acquisition of basic
reading skills. About 10 per cent had barely made a start with reading.
It was clear that given the present age of transfer, junior schools and
departments have to be prepared and equipped to continue the specific
teaching of reading skills to a substantial proportion of their first year
children.

Arithmetic ability

Two assessments were made of ability in number work: performance in
a problem arithmetic test; and the teacher's rating of number work on
a five-point scale which stressed insight and understanding, rather than
mechanical or rote ability.

There was evidence that in problem arithmetic ability boys of this
age are superior to girls. The ratings indicated that in terms of understanding number work there are more boys of above average ability
but there is no difference between the sexes in the proportions of average
and below average ability.

Other abilities

As rated by their teachers, the girls showed better 'oral ability' and more
'creativity' than the boys. On the other hand the boys were judged by
their teachers to have more 'knowledge of the world around'.

Special educational treatment

More than 5 per cent of the children in ordinary schools were receiving
special educational help because of educational or mental backwardness.
The head-teachers considered that a further 8 per cent would have
benefited from such help.

The head-teachers considered that about 2 per cent of the children
would have benefited from special schooling at that time. This result
appeared to reflect a need felt by head-teachers for earlier transfer to
special schools than is the practice at present.

Contacts between schools and parents

While the great majority of the children were at schools in which there
was some form of organised contact between the school and the parents,

more than four out of five were at schools without a parent–teacher association.

Allocation to classes

The allocation of children to classes was done mainly on an age basis. About half of the children were in classes where an attempt had been made to achieve a degree of homogeneity by some form of selective grouping based on age within the year group, on ability or by some other arrangement. Only 5 per cent were in 'family groups' and 7 per cent were in classes which had been 'streamed' by ability.

Age of commencing 'phonics' and 'formal written arithmetic'

Comparisons were made between the practice in England and that in Wales and in Scotland in relation to the age at which the systematic teaching of phonics (letter sounds) was commenced and also the age at which formal written arithmetic was introduced. In all three countries a majority of the children had commenced formal written arithmetic and were receiving some systematic teaching of phonics before the age of six. The children in English schools were introduced to both these aspects of their school work later than those in Wales and in Scotland.

Medical and developmental sex comparisons

Accidents

The results on this sub-sample confirm the view that, in general, boys are more accident-prone than girls. Thus a higher percentage of the boys had had one or more hospital admissions for treatment following road accidents, and for all other accidents and injuries which had not occurred within the home. More boys, too, were reported as having had a head injury with loss of consciousness. For home accidents there was no sex difference.

About 3 per cent of the boys had been admitted to hospital on one or more occasions for treatment following a road accident; as many as 10 per cent had had an accident in the home severe enough to warrant hospital admission; and a similar proportion was reported to have been admitted to hospital for other accidents or injuries sustained outside the home. The corresponding figures for girls, although rather less, were still disconcertingly high, emphasising the need for increased concentration upon accident prevention in childhood.

Upper respiratory infections

Reported past upper respiratory infections showed no sex difference. On the other hand, at the medical examinations, more boys were found to have nasal obstruction, some evidence of nasal or postnasal discharge, or enlarged glands in the neck. The boys were also more often reported to be habitual snorers or mouth breathers.

Psychosomatic and behaviour problems

A history of travel sickness was reported more frequently for girls and there was also evidence that they more often had recurrent abdominal pain.

Boys more frequently showed a history of tics or habit spasms, breath holding, head banging or 'rocking'. Boys had more often attended child guidance clinics.

Convulsions

There was some evidence that boys had more fits in the first year of life but not after this period.

Speech

A history of stammer and of other speech difficulty was reported more often in boys; on examination, more boys were assessed as being not fully intelligible during the speech testing and there was also some evidence of a higher incidence of observed stammer. Fewer boys were reported to have been 'talking' (i.e. 'joining two words') by the age of two years. It is not surprising that more of the boys had already attended for speech therapy by seven years.

Ophthalmological and auditory conditions

No sex differences were found for auditory or visual acuity. However, more girls than boys were found to have latent squint on examination.

Congenital malformations

A history of 'port-wine stains' of the skin was more common in girls and there was evidence of a similar sex difference in the history of 'strawberry naevi'. In addition more of the girls had a history of congenital dislocation of the hip—although numbers were small—and there was some evidence of a similar difference in the history of talipes. On examination, more girls were found to have 'birth marks' but more boys had deformities of the chest and external ear.

Hernia

Boys more often had a history of this condition and more of them had been admitted to hospital for hernia repair. At the medical examinations, the boys were reported more frequently by the medical officers to have inguinal hernia.

Environmental findings

Atypical family situations

Approximately 6 per cent of the children were not living with both of their natural parents. (We now know this to have been an under-estimate biased by late returns which were not included. (See p. 40).

Number of children in family

Approximately 9 per cent were living in households in which they were the only child; 77 per cent in households of two, three or four children; and 14 per cent in households where there were five or more children.

Overcrowding

Approximately 11 per cent of the children in England were living in overcrowded conditions.

House moves

About two-thirds of the children had moved home once or more since they were born. Approximately 13 per cent had moved twice and a further 13 per cent three or more times.

School moves

Since the age of five about 17 per cent of the children had changed school once and about 3 per cent two or more times.

Attendance

Of the 10,645 children for whom this information was available, about 70 per cent were recorded as having a school attendance rate of 90 per cent or higher. About 9 per cent of the sample had a record of below 80 per cent attendance in the current school year.

Parents and schools

Some 57 per cent of parents had approached a member of the schoo staff in the current academic year in order to discuss their children. There was no significant difference between the parents of boys and girls in this respect. Teachers' ratings of parental interest on the other hand seemed to show that the girls' parents were more interested in their children's educational progress than the boys'. However, it is possible that the teachers' ratings may have been influenced to an extent by the better progress of the girls. Of the 26 per cent of children whose teachers had instigated discussion with parents, there were significantly more boys than girls.

Parental aspirations

About 81 per cent of the parents said they would like their children to stay on at school after the minimum school leaving age.

Behaviour and adjustment

On starting at their present school, 94 per cent of the children in 'ordinary' maintained and independent schools in the sample were judged by their teachers to have settled down in school within three months. There was evidence that girls settle down more quickly than boys in infant classes, but in view of the fact that the data were retrospective and may have been influenced by present behaviour, this conclusion was regarded as tentative.

The evidence here was very clear that girls at this age in all categories of school are markedly better adjusted than boys when a relatively crude overall assessment is made in terms of the total score of the Bristol Social-Adjustment Guide. It was noted that this overall assessment may mask other differences between boys and girls when more specific aspects of behaviour are examined. This more detailed analysis is presented on page 146.

Approximately 93 per cent of a sub-sample of 7,985 children in all categories of school were reported by their mothers to be 'happy' in school. There was also a highly significant tendency for more girls to be reported as happy at school than boys.

Percentage figures were given for the reported incidence of nine 'developmental difficulties' for boys and for girls. In only three was there a significant difference between the sexes: there was evidence that more boys than girls are reluctant to go to school; more boys than girls have temper tantrums; and more girls are felt to have poor appetites.

Information was gathered from mothers about fourteen other aspects of children's behaviour.

In all but three items there was a significant difference between the sexes in reported incidence. In general, boys at this age are more often reported to show deviant behaviour at home.

Length of schooling, educational attainment and adjustment in school

Children who commence full-time infant schooling before the age of five are, as they approach the transfer to junior schools or classes some two years later, more advanced educationally and better adjusted in school than those who commence school after the age of five, irrespective of the socio-economic status of their families.

Parental situation and attainment at school

There was evidence from the present Study of an association between parental situation and socio-economic status; there was a consistent tendency for the number of 'atypical' parental situations to increase from Occupational Group 1 through to Occupation Group 5*.

An association was demonstrated between poor reading ability and 'atypical' parental situation which was highly significant for boys and significant for girls.

There was a highly significant association between reading ability and parental situation for Occupation Groups 1 and 2 combined and a significant association in Occupational Group 3; the 'normal' group showed better reading ability. However, there was no such association within Occupational Groups 4 and 5 combined.

Parental approach to school and reading attainment

There is a highly significant tendency for the proportion of parents who have approached the school to decrease from Occupational Group 1 through to Occupational Group 5, although this trend is not wholly consistent.

The differences between the 'Approached' group and the 'Not approached' group are highly significant in relation to reading scores for the boys and for the girls. Boys and girls in the 'Approached' group have better reading ability than in the 'Not approached' group.

The differences tended to be in a similar direction within Occupational Groups for boys and girls in relation to reading scores. The differences between the 'Approached' group and the 'Not approached' group were significant in relation to reading scores for boys and girls separately in Occupational Groups 1 and 3 and for boys in Occupational Group 4.

*

First Report Occupational group	Corresponding Second Report Registrar General's social class
1	I and II
2	III non-manual
3	III manual
4	IV
5	V

References

PRINGLE, M. L. K. and BUTLER, N. R. and DAVIE, R. (1966) *11,000 Seven-Year-Olds*, Longmans.

CENTRAL ADVISORY COUNCIL FOR EDUCATION (1967) *Children and their Primary Schools* (2 volumes) (The 'Plowden Report') H.M.S.O.

MORRIS, J. M. (1959) *Reading in the Primary School*, National Foundation for Educational Research.

4. The parents, the family and the child

Introduction

In early life a great deal of children's development is determined by their learning at home. This is not to overlook the importance of heredity, particularly in relation to physical growth and also for intellectual development; nor to deny the influence of the wider environment of the neighbourhood and of the community. For the young child, however, the home and the family play the major part in drawing out and structuring his abilities, moulding his personality and behaviour, giving direction to his interests and shaping his attitudes.

The relevance of social class in investigating the influence of the home environment has already been discussed in some detail (see p. 2) and the relationship between social class and many aspects of children's development is considered in other chapters.

In this chapter and the following one, attention is focused on particular aspects of the home environment; their relationship to children's educational attainments and adjustment in school; and upon regional differences in these environmental factors. Family and home influences operate in complex and subtle ways. The analysis of the material can take some account of these complexities but a large-scale study is not well equipped to search out the subtleties. These can best be dealt with in smaller studies with their sharper focus and more detailed information. Nevertheless there is a great deal of interest in the broader issues. What is the effect of family size upon children's development? How important for the child are the parents' aspirations, their interest in him and their own educational background and social origins? Are the children of working mothers at all retarded educationally and is their behaviour and adjustment affected? Do poor physical conditions in the home or overcrowding have adverse effects?

In this chapter, aspects of the home environment are considered which might be described as 'parent-centred'. It is concerned with the parents' interests in the child and their aspirations for him; their background and present situation; and the size of the family. The effects of these factors upon the children are examined. In the next chapter, we consider the effects of family mobility upon children's development and also the possible influence of the physical conditions in the home. It hardly needs saying that no hard and fast distinction between these two groups of factors is implied.

Before embarking on a consideration of these questions, it is necessary to underline an important assumption which is relevant to most of the discussions which follow: namely, that there is a sense in which the educational system itself contains a built-in bias in favour of middle-class children. This is not to imply that individual teachers discriminate against working-class children in any personal way but that children from middle-class homes find in the school situation basically the same scale of values as they experience at home. By the time children start school, they have acquired an orientation to the world, embracing norms and attitudes which affect their response to school. Many working-class children will find that these norms and attitudes are in significant respects different from those adopted by the school; they will tend to be judged by standards which are alien to their previous experience.

Swift (1969) discusses the impact upon a child's development of the home and the 'way of life' he learns there. 'How he experiences life (and hence what he learns from it) will be greatly influenced by the ways in which he has been taught to think and to value by the culture (i.e. the "way of life") into which he has been initiated. . . . As a child develops, he constantly adds to his perception of himself those ideas which he learns other people to have about him. He learns that he is a "son", a "brother", quiet, weak, clever, Baptist, and so on. . . . [The child] identifies himself according to the perceptions of reality present in the heads of those around him.' These influence him in turn by 'controlling his ideas of what he may do in any situation and what he can expect of life'. In short it follows that 'what a person does in a particular situation is greatly dependent upon his ideas about what he is and what is expected of him'.

Each child brings these ideas and these expectations to the school situation. If these ideas are reinforced and the expectations confirmed then school will be seen as a natural extension of his world. If on the other hand his expectations are confounded, if his ideas about 'what he is' are at variance with the perceptions of him by this unfamiliar group of adults, he will be at best rather confused and at worst completely disorientated in a world with landmarks that he can scarcely perceive far less understand. These expectations of the child go far deeper than his ordinary fantasy projections of himself into the school situation. They have to do with the way he speaks and is spoken to; with his response to pictorial and written material; his view of the relationship between an adult and a child; and his response to competition and frustration.

To the extent that the school and the individual teachers have certain standards, certain values and certain priorities, a child who tends to conform to these norms will be seen as 'progressing' satisfactorily. Such a child is more likely to come from a middle-class home; he is, as it were, 'on the same wavelength'. Attainment tests at best measure reliably what the author of the test and its users judge to be desirable. Most tests of intelligence are designed essentially to predict future performance in school work; and they stand or fall by their ability to do so. But this future performance is judged by standards which will favour certain social groups. Even 'objective' tests are open to the same influence. There is no such thing as a culture-free test.

The implications of this are not that most judgments and measures of children's development are worthless. Teachers, research workers and others must use some framework as a basis for evaluation. That the framework embodies ideas, attitudes and expectations which are more commonly met in middle-class homes and therefore amongst middle-class children, is perhaps inevitable in our society. However, the fact of this framework must be borne in mind in interpreting the results. If our 'yardsticks' are a little bent, this does not mean we should throw them away—especially if we have no others. But their 'curvilinear characteristics' should not be overlooked!

Family size

The term 'family size' conventionally refers to the number of *children* in the family rather than the total number of people. It is here defined as the number of children of the household under the age of twenty-one years. This definition was chosen because it was felt unlikely that older children of the family would have interacted with the study children in the same fashion as the younger ones. However, the age of twenty-one years is arbitrary.

The fact of an inverse relationship between family size and ability and attainment has been shown by a number of workers (e.g. Douglas, 1964; Nesbit and Entwistle, 1967). A frequently suggested explanation is that children in larger families have less contact with their parents and other adults than do children in smaller families. This, it is thought, might mean that their verbal skills and concepts are slower to develop or are permanently retarded to some degree which in turn creates disadvantages for them in other learning activities. The relatively less attention which a child from a large family will tend to receive from his .parents might affect him in other ways, too. In Swift's (op. cit.) terms, there will be fewer opportunities for him to learn *from adults* what is expected of him and to add to 'his perception of himself'. It might be expected therefore that at school, particularly in the early years, children from large families would be less well adjusted to the essentially adult-centred norms and standards there.

Our analysis therefore sets out to test the conclusion of others that family size is related to educational attainment, and to investigate whether or not it is also associated with adjustment in school at the age of seven. Finally, an idea of the order of magnitude of any effects would be of considerable interest.

A little less than 9 per cent of the children in the study were 'only children' that is, there were no other children in the family under the age of twenty one; about 61 per cent came from two- or three-child families; and 30 per cent were in families of four or more children. There was the expected social class trend, middle-class families tending to be smaller than working-class families. Figure 3 shows the proportion of children in families of four or more in the different social class groups. The proportion in Social Class V was well over twice as high as that in the middle-class groups.

In view of the fact that the proportion of middle-class children in Scotland was much lower than in England or Wales, it was not surprising to find that 37 per cent of the Scottish children lived in families of four or more compared with 29 per cent in England and 30 per cent in Wales. However, when allowance was made for the social class differences, family size in Scotland was still seen to be greater than in England and Wales.

An analysis was therefore needed which would estimate the effects of family size upon reading and arithmetic attainment and social adjustment in school *after allowance had been made* for the effects of social class and country. The analyses which were carried out achieved this result: the *separate* effects of the above factors were estimated after allowing for the effects of all the others. Sex was also included as a factor in the analyses in order to increase the precision of the findings. In Figs 4, 5 and 6 the results of the analyses are represented diagrammatically.

A brief word of explanation about these figures will perhaps be found useful, particularly since this kind of presentation is frequently used in the book. In the analyses for reading and arithmetic (Figs 4 and 5), an estimate has been made of the average scores of children who completed the tests at different times, spread over a period of more than twelve months. This gives a kind of 'yardstick' expressed, for example, in

Figure 3. Percentage of children in families containing four or more children by social class

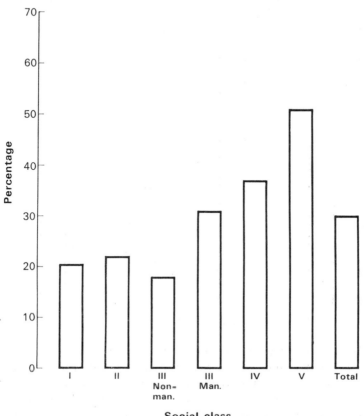

months of reading score, expressed as 'gain in reading age' (Fig. 4) on the left of the figure. The bar charts contained in the figure can therefore be seen in relation to this 'yardstick'. They represent the average difference in the reading test scores of, for instance, boys and girls or of children in Social Classes I and V, when allowances have been made for the other variables in the analysis.

Furthermore, the separate effects shown in the analysis may be added together to give an estimate of the combined effects of the variables used. Thus, the average difference in the reading test scores between, on the one hand, English boys in Social Class V who have four and more brothers or sisters and, on the other hand, Scottish girls in Social Class I who are only children, is equivalent to a gain in reading age of nearly four years.

Figure 4. Family size and reading attainment

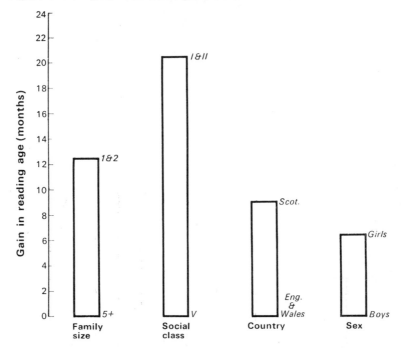

It will be seen that even when these allowances were made, the effect upon reading attainment at the age of seven (Southgate test score) of being in a one- or two-child family compared to a five or more child family, whilst not so large as the social class effect, is still very marked (Fig. 4). It is equivalent to a gain in reading age of about twelve months; and although this estimate should be treated with some caution since it is partly dependent upon the variables included and the groupings chosen, family size is quite clearly a factor which is educationally significant.

The association with arithmetic attainment (Fig. 5), as measured by the problem arithmetic test score, is much smaller and this lends weight to the suggestion that it is in verbal skills that children from large families are most disadvantaged. Furthermore, social adjustment is at least in part effected through contacts with parents and Fig. 6 shows that children from larger families, whatever their social class, sex or country, are less well adjusted in school as measured by the Bristol Social-Adjustment Guide score. There is no convenient yardstick here in contrast to reading and arithmetic attainments, but comparison with the sex difference suggests that the association between family size and adjust-

Figure 5. Family size and arithmetic attainment

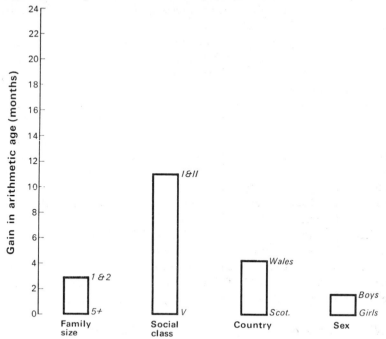

Figure 6. Family size and social adjustment in school

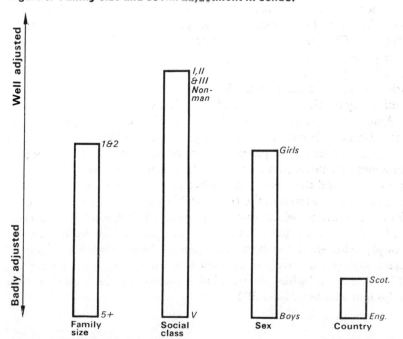

ment in school is large enough to be a very relevant consideration for
educationalists, and for others concerned with the behaviour and adjustment problems of children.

In Chapter 15 the analysis of the effects of family size upon attainment and social adjustment is taken a stage further. Allowance is made
for additional factors but the effects of family size remain. Furthermore,
in these later analyses the separate effects of earlier born and later born
children on the study children are estimated. In Chapter 8 the effects
of family size on children's height is investigated.

The results of the analyses described so far confirm the hypotheses
which were formulated, but nevertheless the reasons advanced must
remain speculative since it is possible that other explanations could
account for the same findings. Might it be, for example, that even
within social classes there are important and relevant differences
between the way of life of parents with larger families apart from
the fact that they are less able to give individual attention to their
children? It is virtually certain that the household income per head
will be smaller and therefore the standard of living will be lower. The
question of the association of family size, household amenities and
overcrowding with attainments and adjustment is examined in the
next chapter.

Where the size of the family is a conscious choice on the part of the
parents, it is reasonable to assume that those with smaller families will
in general be more concerned with their standard of living, perhaps
with the amount of money they can spend on their children, whether
they can afford to support the children in further education and so on.
The parents who *opt* for a large family will have a different set of
priorities, priorities which perhaps are less likely to be achievement
oriented, and less concerned with higher attainment at school or with
conformity to school norms than those of other parents.

Amongst larger families which are not planned in size, apart from
those where religious considerations predominate, there is likely to be
a higher proportion of parents whose attitude is rather feckless and
irresponsible, those who in general do not manage their affairs very
successfully and those who tend to live for the present. This last group
is of particular interest in the context of the earlier discussion about the
framework within which our measures should be seen. The parents
and children will tend to have a scale of values which contrasts quite
sharply with what has been described as 'the middle-class ethic of
postponed gratification'. In Biblical terms they are remembering the
'lilies of the field' whilst the remainder proceeds on the basis that 'God
helps him who helps himself'!

Whatever the reasons for the association between family size, attainment and adjustment—and, as we have seen, they may be complex—it is clear that children from large families are at a considerable disadvantage in school. Further more detailed enquiries should help to clarify the position, but schools can perhaps help by compensating for any retardation of verbal skills and concepts in the classroom programme. Furthermore, although in the analyses the effects of family size were calculated independent of social class, in practice children from large families are also found more frequently in lower social class groups and so they may be disadvantaged in many other ways.

Parents' education and social origins

Common sense suggests that a positive attitude to school will probably be encouraged by those parents who themselves had a good education. On the other hand, common sense also suggests that some of the parents who are most anxious and even enthusiastic about their children's education will be those who regret having missed a better education themselves and want to ensure that their children take advantage of every opportunity. To what extent, then, is school performance related to parents' education?

When the children were seven, information was obtained from the mothers about whether the fathers had stayed on at school beyond the minimum school-leaving age. The same question was asked about the mothers themselves in the original perinatal enquiry. The criterion is a relatively crude one and the group who stayed on at school will include those who went on to a university as well as those who left school after a year or two beyond the minimum age. Among those who left at the minimum age will be some whose jobs involved a considerable amount of training (e.g. in accountancy) and some who re-entered the educational system for retraining, further or higher education. In general terms, however, the parents who stayed on at school will have received more formal education than those who left.

In order to make an analysis more meaningful, it was confined to those children who were living with both natural parents. In all there were 64 per cent of the children both of whose parents had left school at the minimum age. This varied from a mere 12 per cent in Social Class I to as many as 87 per cent in Social Class V.

There was an interesting difference between the picture for fathers and mothers in the social class groups. Amongst the middle-class families, the fathers had more often stayed on at school than their wives, whereas in the working-class families the position was reversed. This may well have arisen because in the working-class groups the mothers more often stayed to take brief commercial courses, whereas those fathers who had further training would have left school to serve an apprenticeship. In middle-class groups a boy's formal education is (or was?) often considered to be of more importance than a girl's.

Information was also obtained about the occupations of both the maternal and paternal grandfathers, which were classified according to whether they were manual or non-manual. Most of the parents whose own background was middle-class will have continued with their formal education, whereas a minority of those with a working-class background will have done so. Parental education will therefore be in part a reflection of social origins.

An analysis was carried out to evaluate the effect of parental education and social origins upon their children's reading and arithmetic attainments and social adjustment in school. It was designed to estimate the effects of these two factors when allowance was made for social class, family size and the sex of the children.

Figure 7. Parental education and children's reading attainment*

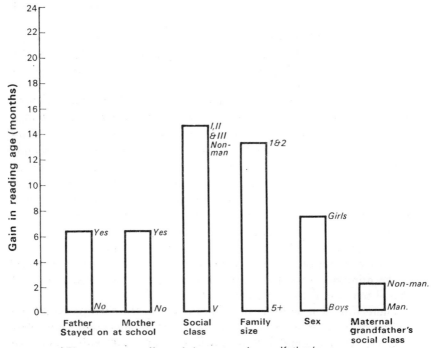

* There was no effect of the paternal grandfather's
  occupation upon the children's reading attainment

Figure 8. Parental education and children's arithmetic attainment*

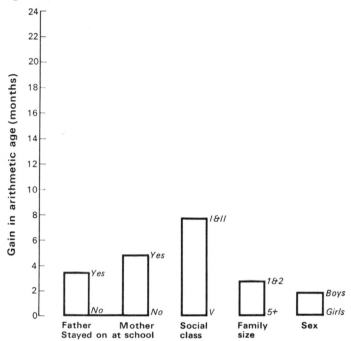

* There was no effect of either the paternal or maternal
grandfather's occupation upon the arithmetic attainment

The results for reading attainment (Fig. 7) indicate that both the
mother's education and the father's are of considerable importance.
The effect of each is equivalent to approximately six months gain in
reading age in the context of this analysis. In contrast the father's social
origins has no effect when allowance is made for the other factors. It
is interesting, however, that the effect of the mother's social origins,
although quite small, is still present. All these effects are small, of
course, in relation to the effects of the *present* social class of the family,
and its size.

In arithmetic (Fig. 8) neither parents' social origins show any effect
but their educational background is still an important factor. This
shows a greater effect than family size, although present social class still
stands out as the most potent predictor.

Again for social adjustment (Fig. 9), the parents' social origins are
in general of little or no consequence. Parental education shows some
residual effect but this is quite small in comparison with social class,
sex and family size.

Figure 9. Parental education and children's social adjustment in school*

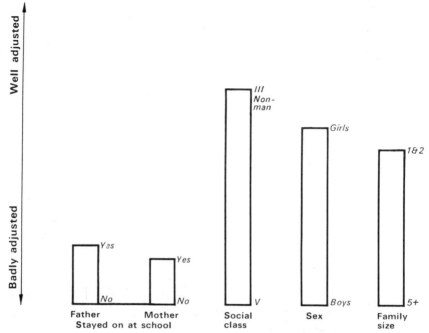

*There was no effect of either the paternal or maternal
grandfather's occupation upon the social adjustment score

Perhaps the most surprising finding is that when allowance is made
for other relevant factors, the parents' social origins are of little or no
importance in predicting their children's school attainments—at least
in reading and arithmetic. Does this mean that we are living in an age
when 'equality of opportunity' is more than a catchphrase and when the
social origins of parents are largely irrelevant to their children's educational achievement? On the basis of other evidence it is perhaps more
likely to mean that our society was (or is?) so static socially that the
parents' present social class and their education can virtually be
equated with their social origins, so that a knowledge of their social
origins is superfluous in predicting their children's achievement. (For
example see Floud, Halsey and Martin (1956)).

However, it is clear from the analysis that parents' *education* has an
important positive effect on their children's development even when
allowance is made for other factors. This finding poses a number of
intriguing questions. Can it be attributed to the education itself and the
attitudes which this engenders? Educationalists no doubt would like
to think so. Or is the explanation that parents who stay on at school

are more intelligent—at least in an academic framework—and that the relevant genes are passed on to their offspring? Perhaps parents who stayed on at school, already had certain attitudes, for example towards school and, more generally, towards academic pursuits and towards authority, which predispose them to stay on. In this case the relevance of the extended education would be that it identifies parents with certain attitudes, which are acquired by their children, who are then better placed to take advantage of schooling in their first two years or so.

Parental interest in their children's education

Three measures of parental interest were used: the teacher's rating; whether or not the parents had visited the school to discuss their child; and the parents' aspirations for the child. The question of the parents' contacts with the school is discussed in another context in Chapter 11.

The teachers' ratings were made on a four-point scale, separately for mothers and fathers. In all, 36 per cent of the mothers were said to be 'very interested', whilst 15 per cent showed 'little or no interest'. The proportion of fathers said to be 'very interested' was much smaller (25 per cent). However, it is difficult to draw firm conclusions from this since there was a large number of fathers about whom the teachers could express no opinion.

The schools were asked to indicate whether parents had taken the initiative to discuss their child, even briefly, with any member of the teaching staff. Overall, 56 per cent of the parents had made this approach.

The parental interview included a question about the parents educational aspirations for their child. The majority of parents (82 per cent) said that they wanted their seven-year-old children to remain at secondary school beyond the minimum school leaving age. This figure, of course, needs to be treated with caution. Some parents would have felt that their child was too young for them to give a considered reply. Some no doubt would have been influenced in their reply by what they thought the interviewer wanted to hear.

The social class differences for all three measures of parental interest are predictably large. For example, the proportion of children in Social Class I whose parents had taken the initiative to discuss them with a member of the school staff was 76 per cent. The corresponding proportion in Social Class V was 43 per cent.

An analysis was also carried out of national differences in parental interest as measured by the teachers' ratings. The apparent differences between England, Wales and Scotland and between the northern and southern zones of England proved to be reflections of the social class differences between these regions. Of course, it is likely that these (subjective) ratings by the teachers were influenced to some extent by the prevailing level of parental interest in the locality and the region. How else is a Scottish teacher, say, to judge the interest of particular parents except against the interest shown by Scottish parents in general? To this extent, then, the lack of difference in the regional analyses, when allowance was made for social class may be misleading.

The proportion of parents who stated that they wished their child to stay on at school contrasts so sharply with the proportion of children who actually stay on that one wonders what the explanation is. For example, of all the children in maintained and non-maintained schools who were thirteen years of age in 1965, only one-third were still at school in 1968 (i.e. at age sixteen).

Is there going to be a substantial increase in the proportion of children staying on at school within the next few years? Or do parents have unrealistic aspirations when their children are younger? Are economic pressures too great for many parents to resist the chance of an extra wage? Is it, perhaps, really the children's decision and not the parents? Subsequent follow-ups of the children should give answers to these questions, which have important implications for educational policy and provision.

The social class differences in parental interest are possibly somewhat inflated. The teachers' ratings may have been a little biased. That is to say that in so far as there was any tendency to guess at the level of parental interest on inadequate evidence, this would have favoured the middle-class children. A parental initiative to speak with a teacher would come more readily from middle-class parents. Such parents might also be more likely to report high aspirations because it would be expected of them. Nevertheless, even when some allowance is made for any artificial discrepancies, the social class differences remain depressingly large. In Chapter 11, some implications of this situation for parent–school contacts are discussed.

Parental situation

Unfortunately, not all children have two or even one parent to show an interest in them. In all, 400 of the children (2·8 per cent) were living in households with no male head.

The total proportion of children who were not living with both 'natural' parents was 7·8 per cent. This proportion is larger than that shown in our first report (p. 23) due no doubt in part to the fact that a rather higher percentage of children figuring in the 'late returns' were disadvantaged in one way or another. In addition, however, the first report did not include the Scottish children, amongst whom were a comparatively large number (8·8 per cent) of children who were not living with both natural parents. The proportion of such children in Wales (6·1 per cent) was lower than in England (7·6 per cent).

Children not living with both natural parents are usually regarded as being at some disadvantage, with, perhaps, the exception of children adopted at a very early age. Children from broken homes are frequently mentioned in the literature—as well as in the courts and elsewhere—as being at risk of behaviour and other difficulties. The argument runs that normal development is very dependent on satisfactory relationships at home; and where such relationships are disrupted and disturbed, tensions are likely to be increased and as a consequence educational and/ or emotional development will suffer. Of course, satisfactory relationships are not necessarily absent where a natural parent is missing, nor are they guaranteed by the presence of both natural parents.

Most of the research interest and effort (e.g. Trasler, 1962; Morris, 1966; Gibson, 1969) has been centred on the link between 'broken homes' and later difficulties in children. However, as was mentioned in Chapter 1, by no means all such children show evidence of difficulties. For example, in our first report it was shown that only a little over a fifth of such children were found to be poor readers. This, of course, is only one aspect of development and the longer term picture cannot yet be seen. However, quite clearly, it is not simply the fact of a broken home which causes the trouble; it is the *impact* of the situation upon the child which is important. And in order to investigate these problems fully, it is at least as important to consider why many children from broken homes do *not* show permanent ill effects.

In this context the analyses carried out for our first report are of particular interest. The group of children living in an atypical family situation (i.e. without both natural parents) contained more poor readers than the 'normal' group. On the other hand, the former group also contained relatively more working-class children. When the comparison was repeated within social class groups, the children in an atypical parental situation in middle-class families or in skilled manual working-class families were still shown to be at some disadvantage. In Social Classes IV and V, however, there was no difference in reading performance.

Does this mean that a broken home in general has little or no impact upon children in semi-skilled and unskilled working-class homes? Or is it that children in such homes are relatively disadvantaged in so many ways that the effects of this one additional difficulty cannot be isolated so readily? Is the pattern of life in Social Class IV and V families such that any potential adverse effects of the loss of a parent (or spouse) are more readily mitigated by support from the extended family group or by friends and neighbours?

The *long-term* effects of broken homes on children's development are of most interest but already at seven years of age there is a marked association with reading attainment. What is known about the effects of early failure in school suggests that this may be self-reinforcing unless remedial action is taken. The tentative evidence so far produced, however, indicates that children from Social Class IV and V homes are *not*, in general, more likely to be educationally backward if they are living in an atypical parental situation.

The implications of this last finding are that research is urgently needed to confirm the results in different areas of development and at different ages. These should be linked to more detailed observational studies of what actually happens in different social groups when one of the parents disappears from the family circle (e.g. Marris, 1958). Do others help and support the remaining parent? Does she (or he) re-marry more quickly in certain groups? The situation is analogous to, say, a medical finding that some groups in the population are relatively immune to a particular disease or condition. The investigation of the reasons may well have implications for treatment of the disease through-out the population.

Children of working mothers

For most of this century, apart from increases in times of war, women have constituted about one-third of the work force, a figure which is rising slowly but not startlingly. What is rising fast is the proportion of women workers who are married (Hunt, 1968). Many social commentators have greeted this increase with dismay largely because of its alleged effect upon children.

The assumption behind this attitude is that children will develop best if their mother's time is spent in the home and on the family rather than on paid work outside the home; and that if the mother does work, the older the child is when she starts, the better it is for that child. This view was echoed in a study by Goodacre (1968), who asked teachers what they considered were desirable home conditions. A non-working mother was mentioned in a high proportion of answers.

Not all public comment agrees with this view; a definite note of protest underlies these remarks of a writer in the *Guardian* (3 November, 1969): 'At least once a week, inspired by anything from equal pay for women to a particularly juvenile delinquent, some judge, M.P., professor, psychiatrist, rector or proctor can be counted upon to rise, accuse the working mother and advocate renewed effort in promoting home-making as a talent.'

Home-making probably strikes most people as a 'talent' worth promoting but is it necessarily incompatible with working? Perhaps there are dangers in over-emphasizing the needs of the home and the family. Certainly some observers warn that there are dangers in full-time motherhood: Rossi (1964), for example: 'I suspect that the things women do for and with their children have been needlessly elaborated to make motherhood a full-time job. Unfortunately, in this very process the child's struggle for autonomy and independence, for privacy and the right to worry things through for himself are subtly reduced by the omnipresent mother.'

Here, then, is a controversy about children's development, the implications of which are both social and economic. Are there any facts with which to augment the hearsay evidence? What support may the protagonists discover in research findings? Stolz (1960) concluded that the results were so contradictory that almost any point of view could find some support. The lack of any consensus was attributed to the failure of the research workers to take account fully—if at all—of the relevant factors. These would include, for example, social class, family size, the age of the child, the duration of the work and the standard of alternative care.

Clearly, failure to take account of these factors could lead to conflicting results. For example, analysis of our results showed that working mothers were more in evidence in the less skilled social class groups, so that on this basis their children might be expected to compare unfavourably in school performance with those of non-working mothers. Secondly, however, working mothers tended to have *smaller* families and, as has been shown, children from small families do *better* at school than those in large families. Thirdly, although this was not specifically examined, it seemed reasonable to assume that the group of working mothers would more often contain widows and wives separated from their husbands. Again, it has been shown that children living in atypical parental situations are at some disadvantage educationally.

The analysis was therefore designed to make allowance for social class and family size differences and was confined to children living with both natural parents.

When interviewed the mothers were asked whether they had been in paid work outside the home; whether any such work had been undertaken before or after the child had started school at five years; and whether it was full-time, part-time or temporary. Work of less than one month's duration was discounted. The proportions of all mothers who worked full-time both before the child started school and afterwards were fairly constant at around 9 or 10 per cent. On the other hand, the proportions who took part-time or temporary work before the child started school (20 per cent) was much smaller than those who had such work afterwards (34 per cent). Overall, some 52 per cent of the mothers had never worked, and 48 per cent had worked at some time.

The results of the analyses of the effect of mothers working upon children's reading and arithmetic attainment and social adjustment in school are presented in Figs 10, 11 and 12. These included only those children with both natural parents and took into account the different work situations, although the part-time and temporary workers were grouped together.

The results of the reading analysis (Fig. 10) indicate that when allowance has been made for the other factors there is a clear association between mothers working before children start school and reading attainment at the age of seven. The association for working after children start school is smaller. Even the former result, although clear, shows a

Figure 10. Mother's working and children's reading attainment

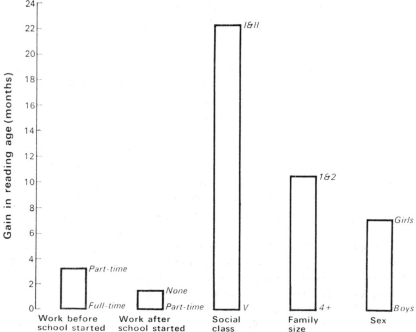

Figure 11. Mother's working and children's arithmetic attainment*

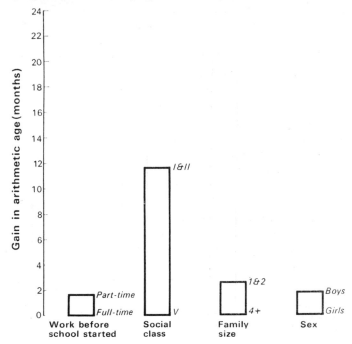

*There was no effect of the mother working after school started upon the children's arithmetic attainment

relatively small effect when compared with the effects of social class and family size and is also smaller than the sex effect. Within the context of this analysis and the groupings chosen it represents a loss in reading age of approximately three months for those children whose mothers worked full-time before they started school.

The results of the analysis of arithmetic attainment (Fig. 11) fail to indicate an effect of mothers working after their children started school. The result for mothers working before their children started school shows a small effect, equivalent to one month's progress in arithmetic.

What of the social adjustment of the children of working mothers (Fig. 12)? The children whose mother worked before they started school were no worse adjusted than children of non-working mothers. However, those whose mother worked after they started school were shown to be less well adjusted than the others. The effect, as can be seen, is quite small in relation to the effects of the other factors.

Of course, the analyses do not answer unequivocally all of the questions raised earlier. No account could be taken of the quality or even

Figure 12. Mother's working and children's social adjustment in school

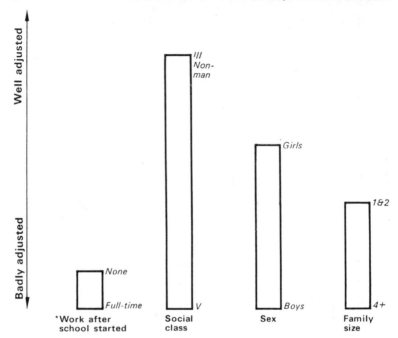

*There was no effect of the mother working *before* school
started upon the children's social adjustment

adequacy of any arrangements for substitute care whilst the mothers
were working. Hardly any account was taken of the situation and
characteristics of the mothers except in terms of their social class and
the size of their families. The information about their work histories
was relatively crude.

However, it is clear that, in general, the children of working mothers
do not show any marked ill-effects at the age of seven in terms of their
attainment and adjustment in school. It may be that any important
ill-effects will manifest themselves at later ages but this seems unlikely
since a younger child is more vulnerable to environmental and other
stresses. It may also be that the children's behaviour or adjustment *at
home* suffers and this must for the moment remain an open question.
Analysis of this is planned for the future.

The two clear results which did emerge pose some interesting questions. Why should the children of mothers who work before they start
school show no signs of poor adjustment in school, whilst the children of
mothers who work after they start school do show small signs? If the

important element in the situation were maternal deprivation, surely the opposite would be expected since younger children are more vulnerable. Might it be that the child with a working mother before he starts school has become adjusted to this situation by the age of seven? If so, the difficulties of the children to whom a working mother is a fairly recent phenomenon might be temporary. Or is it that working mothers with a pre-school child are forced to make arrangements for substitute care, whereas mothers who work later may tend more often to resort to a 'latch-key' situation, leaving the children somewhat insecure?

The rather poorer reading performance of the children whose mothers work before they start school may perhaps be explained by reduced opportunities for close contact with an adult. In terms of the development of verbal skills and concepts many of the conventional child care arrangements compare unfavourably with the 'omnipresent mother'.

However, to return to the overall picture it seems clear that many of the accusations laid at the door of the working mother are ill-founded. Such effects as have been noted here are relatively small.

References

DOUGLAS, J. W. B. (1964) *The Home and the School*, MacGibbon & Kee.

FLOUD, J., HALSEY, A. H. and MARTIN, F. M. (1956) *Social Class and Educational Opportunity*, Heinemann.

GIBSON, H. B. (1969) 'Early delinquency in relation to broken homes', *Journal of Child Psychology and Psychiatry*, **10**, 194–204.

GOODACRE, E. (1968) *Teachers and their Pupils' Home Backgrounds*, National Foundation for Educational Research.

HUNT, A. (1968) *A Survey of Women's Employment*, H.M.S.O.

MARRIS, P. (1958) *Widows and their Families*, Routledge & Kegan Paul.

MORRIS, J. M. (1966) *Standards and Progress in Reading*, National Foundation for Educational Research.

NESBIT, J. D. and ENTWISTLE, N. J. (1967) 'Intelligence and Family Size', *B.J. Ed. Psych.*, **37**, 188–193.

TRASLER, G. (1962) *The Explanation of Criminality*, Routledge & Kegan Paul.

ROSSI, A. S. (1964) *Equality Between the Sexes: an immodest proposal*, Daedalus.

STOLZ, L. M. (1960) 'Effects of maternal employment on children', *Child Development*, No. 31.

SWIFT, D. F. (1969) *The Sociology of Education*, Routledge & Kegan Paul.

3

5. Family moves and housing conditions

Introduction

We consider first the mobility of the children's families, that is to say their change of home. This sometimes meant changes of school for the children, and this question is discussed too. Finally, the effects of housing conditions upon children's educational attainments and social adjustment are examined.

Family moves

It is a common occurrence for a family to move home; indeed, as will be shown, the majority of the children in the study had experienced at least one such move by the age of seven years.* A much smaller proportion of children had changed school by this time, since most children would have been at school for only two or three years. Also a substantial proportion of house moves were made within a local area. However, a change of school whilst children are at the infant stage is still relatively common.

Such changes can be unsettling for children but it seems a reasonable assumption that any difficulties which may arise—be they educational, psychological or social—will normally be of a transient nature. Indeed, in some circumstances a change of environment may be beneficial, particularly where the new environment is 'better' in significant respects than the old one. A succession of changes, however, is likely to threaten a child's feelings of security with implications for his emotional and social adjustment and, where changes of school are also involved, his educational progress may be affected.

No attempt is made here to investigate such effects, although analyses along these lines are planned for the future. The results presented are

---

* The average age of the children when the mothers were interviewed was approximately seven years six months.

of a descriptive nature and include a scrutiny of the social class and regional variations in mobility.

Some 64 per cent of the children had moved house at least once; 27 per cent had moved more than once; and 7 per cent had moved four or more times. There was no consistent social class trend in these findings but 73 per cent of the children in Social Class I had experienced at least one house move and only 63 per cent in Social Class II and IV. However, where there was no male head of the household, the proportion (71 per cent) was comparable with that of children in Social Class I.

The pattern in England showed increased mobility in the southern regions. On the other hand, the proportion of children in Scotland who had moved (67 per cent) was rather higher than in England (64 per cent) or Wales (60 per cent).

The number of 'frequent' moves (four or more) is of considerably more interest since, as has been suggested, this is more likely to have implications for children's development. Here, the children living in households with no male head stand out as a particularly vulnerable group; approximately 15 per cent of them were 'frequent' movers. Social Class I children (10 per cent) and Social Class V children (9 per cent) shared the characteristic of frequent moving and contrasted with the children in the other social classes where the proportions were roughly equal at about 6 per cent.

In general, moves are more likely to unsettle children, as well as parents, if they are made out of the local area. However, there is some difficulty in arriving at a satisfactory criterion of what constitutes a 'local area'. The way of life of some families (including the availability of a car) may be such that a move of a few miles away may involve considerable social readjustment, whereas for others a rather more distant move may still be compatible with maintaining former friends. As a supplementary question, therefore, the mothers were asked how many of the family moves were beyond a point 'where personal contact with former friends could be readily maintained'. Overall, nearly two-thirds (62 per cent) of the movers remained within range of former friends. The results showed a consistent social class trend. Thus, stable friendships were most frequently possible for unskilled manual workers' children (Social Class V) of whom only 27 per cent had moved out of the local area and least likely for the children of professional families (Social Class I) where the proportion was 63 per cent.

The proportion of children who change *school* by their last term of infant schooling must clearly be smaller than the above since this will be a reflection of family moves only in the children's last two or three years. Some 20 per cent had changed school at least once and 3 per cent had attended three or more schools. As one might expect, the children who change school come proportionately more often from middle-class than working-class families. There was also a higher proportion in England (21 per cent) than in Scotland (16 per cent) or Wales (17 per cent).

Comparisons with other studies are extremely difficult since the age of the child when the information was collected is critical: the older the child the longer the period during which moves could be made. The definition of a 'move' is also extremely important. Douglas (1964) found that, predictably, family moves are more frequent during children's earlier years. Some 67 per cent of his national sample of children had moved by the age of eleven years. It would, however, be surprising if mobility had not increased since the 1950s.

The implications of the relatively high proportion of frequent moves among children living in households with no male head clearly needs investigation. Is this one of the significant factors in influencing the development of children from 'broken homes'?

Household amenities and overcrowding in the home

In this section attention is focused on some aspects of the physical environment in the children's homes. It must be a matter of concern to everyone that some children grow up in conditions which are lacking the basic amenities of a bathroom, hot water supply, indoor lavatory and a garden or yard in which to play. The actual space which children have within the home is also important in terms of their need—and their parents' need—for some privacy and for opportunities for following individual interests as well as sharing in those of the family.

First, the size of the overcrowding problem is considered and the study results are compared with figures from the 1966 census in England and Wales. The facts are disturbing.

The prevalence of overcrowding

A number of different definitions of overcrowding have been used by different agencies. The one selected for use in the present study was that adopted by the Registrar General for the 1961 census. The total number of persons in the household, irrespective of age or sex, is divided by the number of living rooms and bedrooms in the house; this ratio is used as an index of crowding. A kitchen is counted as a room for this purpose only if it is used for eating (or sleeping). Any child living in a household with more than 1·5 persons per room is deemed to be overcrowded by this definition. This is in no way a luxury standard; indeed, the Milner

Holland report *Housing in Greater London* (H.M.S.O., 1965) considered it to lag 'far behind what is regarded as acceptable even by average sections of the community'. For example, a family of a husband, wife and four children having two bedrooms and two 'living' rooms would *not* be overcrowded by this standard.

Some 15 per cent—or more than one in seven—of the study children were in 1965 living in overcrowded conditions at home. The regional picture (Fig. 13) shows that in Scotland the situation was much worse than in other parts of Britain; 39 per cent—more than one in three—of the Scottish children were living in overcrowded conditions. There are also some striking variations between the English regions: for example, the proportion of overcrowded children in the northern region (18 per

Figure 13. Percentage of children overcrowded by region and country

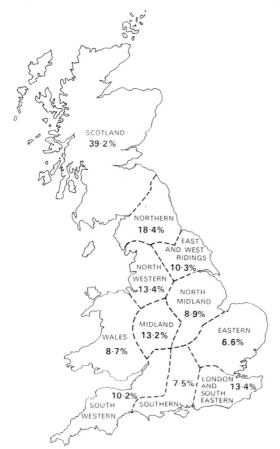

cent) was nearly two and a half times as large as that in the eastern region (7 per cent). In relation to the total picture the problem in Wales was a modest one (9 per cent).

Not surprisingly, overcrowding shows a marked social class trend: the lower the social class, the more likely is a child to live in an over-crowded home. In Social Class I, for instance, the figure was 1 per cent, whilst in Social Class V it was 37 per cent. Children who were living in a whole house were better off for space (12 per cent overcrowded) than those who lived in flats (31 per cent overcrowded) or rooms (54 per cent overcrowded). Somewhat unexpectedly, the children of council house tenants were as likely to be overcrowded (23 per cent) as those who lived in privately rented accommodation (22 per cent). The children in owner-occupied accommodation fared best (5 per cent).

Despite widespread interest in housing conditions as they affect both individuals and public policy, there has until recently been no com-prehensive national information available other than from the census, although various estimates have been made. In addition, very little indeed is published on the housing conditions of particular groups within the community (such as families with young children, or single women) or on the extent to which their special needs are being met. However, it is clear that, in general, childless couples and people living alone will less often live in overcrowded conditions; and a number of smaller scale studies have confirmed that households with at least three children under sixteen years are much more likely to be short of space than other households (e.g. Gray and Russell, 1962).

In view of this, it is not surprising to find that the extent of over-crowding amongst all persons in the 1966 census (H.M.S.O., 1969) was much smaller than the figures obtained in our study, which were based upon a sample of children. The census overcrowding figure of 3·2 per cent of persons in Great Britain (2·5 per cent for England and Wales; 9·9 per cent for Scotland) is, however, also smaller for another reason: the definition of a 'room' is different. In the study—as in the 1961 census—the kitchen was only included as a room where it was used for eating or sleeping in, whereas in the 1966 census, *all* kitchens were counted as rooms. This new, less stringent definition has the effect, of course, of lowering the overcrowding figures.

In order to obtain comparable national figures for overcrowding amongst children of primary school age, it was arranged for a special tabulation to be prepared for the study by the General Register Office. This showed that among *children* aged five to ten years the extent of overcrowding in England and Wales in 1966 was more than twice as high (5·8 per cent) than for all *persons* (2·5 per cent).

The above figure of 5·8 per cent of primary school-age children over-crowded in the 1966 census when compared with the corresponding one from the study (in England and Wales) of approximately 12 per cent in 1965 indicates that the new census definition of a room reduces the overcrowding figures by about a half.

Amenities in the home

In Scotland, although the rate of overcrowding was very high, house-holds were in general well supplied with basic amenities. In Wales, the converse was true. There was a relatively low overcrowding rate but overall the Welsh children were worse off than their Scottish and English peers for indoor lavatories and bathrooms. One in every four Welsh children, for example, did not have an indoor lavatory at home.

In general, however, the more crowded the home, the less likely it was to have the three 'basic' amenities: a hot water supply, a bathroom and an indoor lavatory. In the least crowded group (those children living at a density of one person per room or less), 86 per cent also had sole use of all these amenities. Amongst the most crowded group (more than two persons per room) only 51 per cent had sole use of all these amenities.

As with overcrowding, the availability of amenities showed a marked social class trend. Approximately 93 per cent of the children from Social Classes I and II had the sole use of all the above amenities, whereas in Social Class V less than two-thirds of the children did so.

Less than 1 per cent of the mothers reported that they either lacked or had to share cooking facilities. Overall, nearly 90 per cent of the children were in households with the sole use of a garden or yard, 6 per cent had to share this amenity and 4 per cent had no garden or yard in which to play. However, the regional results showed wide variations; gardens and yards were notably less common in Scotland and in the London and South East Region of England.

All the results discussed, particularly those for overcrowding, are disturbing. Quite apart from any readily measurable effects of over-crowding in terms of children's school attainment or adjustment, the impact of a lack of space upon the quality of life must surely call for strenuous efforts to remedy the present situation. As was mentioned previously, even by the earlier 1961 definition of a room, the standard of 1·5 persons per room was stated by an authoritative source some years ago to be unacceptable 'even by average sections of the community' (H.M.S.O., 1965). One in eleven of the children in Wales, one in eight children in England and more than one in three children in Scotland were living in conditions at home which failed to meet this standard.

The relationship between overcrowding, lack of household amenities, educational attainment and social adjustment

Poor housing is often mentioned as one of the contributory causes of school failure. In the Introduction to *Equality* (Tawney, 1964 edition), Professor R. M. Titmuss states: 'We delude ourselves if we think we can equalise the social distribution of life chances by expanding educational opportunities while millions of children live in slums without baths, decent lavatories, leisure facilities, room to explore and space to dream.'

It is not difficult to think of plausible reasons why there should be a relationship between overcrowding and poor performance at school. Children with less space at home in which to play, to work or to read and, perhaps, whose sleep is interrupted by other members of the household, are less likely to give a good account of themselves at school. Furthermore, as has been shown, families living in overcrowded conditions are more likely to lack basic household amenities and they are more often found in the less skilled occupational groups. In fact, 'crowding keys in with other deprivations, each reinforcing the other'

Figure 14. Overcrowding, lack of amenities, and reading attainment

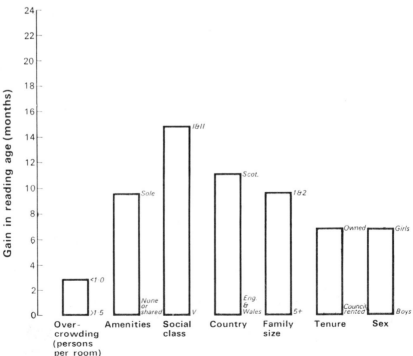

Figure 15. Overcrowding, lack of amenities, and arithmetic attainment

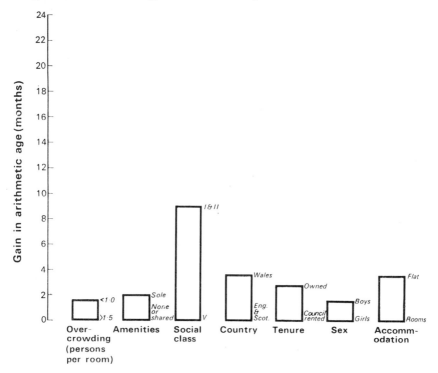

(Schorr, 1964). However, it is this very interrelatedness which makes so difficult the task of isolating any effects of overcrowding or of lack of basic household amenities as such.

In the analyses which follow, allowance has been made for the following factors: social class; sex; country (England, Wales, Scotland); type of accommodation (whole house, flat, rooms); tenure (owner-occupied, council tenancy, privately rented); and number of children. The question which is posed, then, is: when allowance has been made for the effects of these factors, what are the effects of overcrowding in the home and poor household amenities upon children's attainment and adjustment in school?

In Figs 14, 15 and 16 the results of the analyses are presented. The estimated effects of having sole use of the three 'basic' amenities (hot water, bathroom and indoor lavatory) have been added together and appear as one factor.

The results for reading attainment (Fig. 14) indicate that both overcrowding and basic amenities are important. The effect of overcrowding

Figure 16. Overcrowding, lack of amenities, and social adjustment

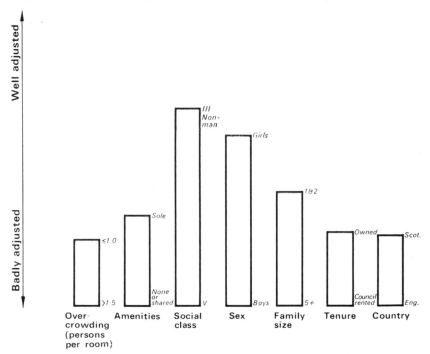

is equivalent to two or three months retardation in reading age in the context of this analysis. The effect of absence—or shared use—of all basic amenities is equivalent to about nine months' retardation in reading age.

In the case of arithmetic attainment (Fig. 15), the effects were smaller, being equivalent to about one and a half months' retardation in arithmetic attainment for overcrowding, and some two months for absence of basic amenities.

For social adjustment in school (Fig. 16), as measured by the Bristol Social-Adjustment Guide score, the effect of a lack of sole use of the three basic amenities was approximately half that of social class. The effect of overcrowding was rather smaller than the 'amenities effect'.

Are we to conclude then, that while the effects of lack of basic amenities on reading attainment and social adjustment are considerable, the effects of overcrowding are relatively modest? If so, one important consideration would be overlooked, namely the relationship between overcrowding and family size. The points raised are of a rather complex nature and need not concern us in detail here (see appendix). However, the central point is that whereas all of the other factors (social class, etc.) are logically independent of overcrowding, family size is not. This is because the number of children in the household forms part of the basis for the crowding index. There are good grounds for estimating the effect of overcrowding without making separate allowance for family size in the analysis. When this is done, the effect of overcrowding upon reading attainment is equivalent to approximately nine months' retardation in reading age, i.e. the same order of effect as for lack of the basic amenities. For social adjustment, the effect of overcrowding in the amended analysis is much larger than the lack of amenities effect and approaches the sex effect in size.

The results have demonstrated clearly the relationships between poor housing amenities and overcrowding on the one hand and on the other hand educational performance and social adjustment in school at the age of seven. These findings are particularly disturbing since poor housing conditions and overcrowding tend to 'key in' with one another and with other disadvantaging circumstances.

It would, of course, be naive to assume a direct causal relationship between, say, lack of hot water in the household and children's reading attainment. But poor housing conditions may well lead to a low standard of physical health; depression and irritability in parents; and may produce a feeling of 'distance' from the more privileged sections of society (with which the school may be identified).

Thus, a *combination* of adverse environmental circumstances may well have a deleterious effect on children's development. It follows that the solution to the problem should be seen 'in the round' and tackled in this light. Simply building more houses is unfortunately not enough. Spare houses in inaccessible areas or an 'overall housing surplus' are of no use to the semiskilled and unskilled workers living and working in the decaying centres of our major cities where the worst housing conditions are found. The housing problem is inextricably entwined with the low-wage problem, the employment situation and the availability of public transport.

However, an improvement in housing conditions and other environmental circumstances cannot be achieved overnight, and so attention needs to be given to ways of ameliorating their effects. The Plowden Committee (H.M.S.O., 1967) suggested a programme of educational compensation through 'educational priority areas'. Such schemes are unlikely to be fully effective until the ways in which children are influenced by adverse environmental circumstances are better understood. Further research in this area, therefore, is urgently needed.

References

CENTRAL ADVISORY COUNCIL FOR EDUCATION (1967) *Children and their Primary Schools*, (The Plowden report), 2 vols, H.M.S.O.

DOUGLAS, J. W. B. (1964) *The Home and the School*, MacGibbon & Kee.

GENERAL REGISTER OFFICE (1969) *1966 Sample Census, Housing Tables*, H.M.S.O.

GRAY, P. G. and RUSSELL, R. (1962) *The Housing Situation in 1960*, C.O.I.

HOUSING AND LOCAL GOVERNMENT, MINISTRY OF, Committee on Housing in Greater London (1965) *Housing in Greater London* (Milner-Holland report), H.M.S.O.

SCHORR, A. L. (1964) *Slums and Social Insecurity*, Nelson.

TAWNEY, R. H. (1964) *Equality*, 4th edn rev. Allen & Unwin.

6. The utilisation of medical and other services

Introduction

It is now accepted in Britain that a full range of medical and other services for children should be available within reasonable distance of their homes. Inevitably, urban areas are in general better able to reach this goal but the efforts of early pioneers and their successors, aided by the relatively high density of population in Britain, has meant a good standard over most of the country. However, it is important to discover how much these services are in fact used. Regional variations in the use of services will to some extent reflect the availability of services but they might also reflect regional attitudes. 'Child guidance' might be a more acceptable concept in Cheltenham than in Chorley or *vice versa*. Of course, attitudes will vary within regions too, and an examination of social class differences will also be of considerable interest. Possibly, too, those families who use the services least are the ones who need them most.

The services discussed in this chapter are mostly of a medical or para-medical nature and they range from those concerned exclusively with preventive work to those whose major function is to provide treatment.

Infant welfare clinics

These clinics are provided by local authorities under statute. Advice to mothers and the medical examination and inspection of pre-school children is given without charge; and immunisation against polio, diphtheria, tetanus, whooping cough, smallpox, and in recent years, measles is carried out. Welfare foods, i.e. dried milk powder and vitamin preparations are sold at subsidised prices. These clinics are essentially prophylactic and diagnostic; problems outside their scope are referred to appropriate agencies including, of course, general practitioners.

Who in fact uses these facilities? Do they, in an age of improving infant health, still serve a meaningful and useful role?

With changing patterns of need, there has been a shift in emphasis from treatment to prevention. Overfeeding, not underfeeding, has become the new 'malnutrition', although of course, poverty has by no means been conquered yet. Attendance at a local authority clinic is not compulsory, though health visitors are charged with the responsibility of calling on homes where there are young children and encouraging attendance.

According to the mothers' reports, more than three out of every four of the children were taken to infant welfare clinics in their first year; Welsh children being taken most frequently (82 per cent) and Scottish children least frequently (64 per cent). Non-attendance at an infant welfare clinic does not necessarily imply that a child is not receiving full medical attention. Many general practitioners, especially in rural areas, hold 'well baby clinics' on their own premises or, where lists are small, make routine visits to their young patients at home.

The social class pattern showed reduced attendance at both ends of the scale: approximately 75 per cent had attended in Social Classes I and II as well as in IV and V, whereas the proportions in Social Class III (non-manual) and III (manual) were 83 per cent and 79 per cent respectively.

There need be little concern about the relative underuse of clinics amongst Social Class I children: as will be shown later, these children had by far the highest level of immunisation, implying higher attendance at surgeries or home visits by their general practitioners. The same applies to a lesser extent to Social Class II children. However, the relatively low attendance in the semiskilled and unskilled occupational groups together with a lower level of immunisation suggests that as a group these children were not receiving their full entitlement to welfare and medical services.

This finding reinforces the concept that services must not only be available but that people who need them must be actively encouraged to use them. Health visitors, as their title implies, do go out of their way to visit in their own homes those children who are not brought to clinics but we do not have statistics showing how often this was in fact done. The actual attendance at a clinic does have the advantage of a medical examination when necessary, as well as the benefits of social contact with other mothers.

Toddler clinics

The above results relate to the children's attendance at clinics in their first year. Older pre-school children have been termed 'toddlers'.

Generally, mothers are encouraged to attend the same welfare clinics but in a few areas, separate 'toddler-clinics' exist.

After their first birthday, many fewer (56 per cent) of the children continued to attend these clinics. Again, the most frequent attenders were the children in Social Class III (non-manual) and III (manual) and there were poorer attendances from the groups above and below these. However, the children from Social Class V homes appeared to slip back much farther than the other groups with only 47 per cent attendance.

The pattern of attendance as between England, Scotland and Wales was similar to those for infant welfare clinics: the Welsh attended most frequently (65 per cent) and the Scots least (44 per cent). It is interesting that a difference between the northern and southern regions of England, which is seen for infant welfare clinic attendance, appears to widen at the toddler stage. Does this reflect a regional difference in parents' attitudes as the children grow older or has it to do with the better provision of services in the South?

In recent years there has been a movement towards a regular assessment at these clinics of the developmental progress made by children during their early years. Particular stress is laid on the assessment of vision and hearing. It is probable that future use of the clinics will be along these lines with a special attempt being made to focus the welfare element towards children most in need.

Immunisations

In 1958 routine immunisation was offered against diphtheria, whooping cough, smallpox and poliomyelitis. The mothers in the study were not asked how many immunisations their child had had, in view of the seven-year interval between birth and the interview. Enquiry was limited to whether *any* immunisation had been given against smallpox, poliomyelitis or diphtheria respectively. A subsidiary question was included for completion where no immunisation was reported, as to whether the lack of immunisation was due to parental objection. This was affirmed in about one in three of those not immunised, the proportion due to this being the same for each type of immunisation.

Smallpox vaccination

Smallpox vaccination normally requires a single attendance. Three-quarters (77 per cent) of the children had already been vaccinated by seven years of age; there was no sex difference. The highest rate of vaccination was in Social Class I families at 94 per cent; the percentage of children protected against this, one of the cruellest of diseases, fell with declining social class, the lowest rate of vaccination being 66 per cent in Social Class V families. Although fewer of the children in the higher social classes were not immunised, the proportion of parents of *non-immunised* children who actually objected to the procedure being performed, showed a slight downwards trend from high in Social Class I and II to low in Social Class V.

The proportion of the sample reported unvaccinated was only 15 per cent in the East, South East, and Southern regions of England, with a similar figure for Wales (where an epidemic of smallpox in 1962 in South Wales had resulted in a mass vaccination campaign). But the proportion rose progressively going northwards, with a maximum of more than one in three of the children in the North and North Midlands regions being unvaccinated.

Polio immunisation

Killed polio virus (Salk type) given by injection was the method of choice until the late 1950s. Subsequently, oral immunisation has been favoured, using modified living poliovaccine (Sabin). Some 95 per cent of children were reported as receiving one or more immunisations against polio-myelitis, a higher proportion than for smallpox. The fact that 10 per

Figure 17. Percentage of children not immunised against polio by social class

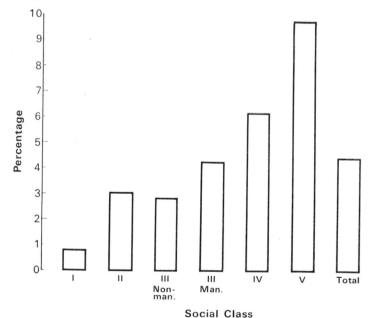

Social Class

cent of the children in Social Class V families against 1 per cent from Social Class I were deprived of the protection that was theirs by right, underlines once again the need for more positive action. (See Fig. 17.) Special efforts appear to have been made in Scotland where 99 per cent of the children were reported as receiving some protection.

Diphtheria immunisation

The proportion reported as receiving some protection against diphtheria immunisation was similar to that for polio, some 6 per cent of the children were reported as being completely unprotected. The social class pattern was again similar to that for polio immunisation. No case of diphtheria actually occurred in the sample but experience has taught the lesson that the disease lurks in wait for the unprotected. Like polio, diphtheria has now passed out of the experience of most parents and interest in protection has to be artificially stimulated by publicity.

The teeth

Many studies have shown that the standard of dental health in primitive communities falls as they become more sophisticated. The decline in dental health accompanies the increase in the use of refined sugars, together with the elimination of the tooth cleansing fibrous foods from the diet.

There is no doubt that simple hygienic measures can play a large part in the preservation of dental health. Despite the advent of a free dental service in 1948 for British children, there remains a paucity of national data from which to evaluate standards of dental health. Valuable information is published in *The Health of the School Child* (H.M.S.O., 1969) in which returns from seven English local authorities are published, showing quite marked regional variations in standards, but there is no further analysis of this information.

Our study included a retrospective enquiry about attendance at dental clinics or private dentists. Current policy dictates a statutory examination of the teeth on entry to the state school system. Children requiring treatment may attend a private dentist or receive treatment under the school service. It was disappointing to find that one in four (23 per cent) of parents reported that their child had never attended any dentist. One can but hope that this is an overestimate and that some parents may have forgotten that their child had an inspection at school. Parents however, are required to be notified of impending dental examinations at school and are encouraged to attend. There was no sex difference in these results but there was a social class trend from 84 per cent attendance in Social Class I to 68 per cent in Social Class V

Figure 18. Percentage of children who had never attended a dentist by social class

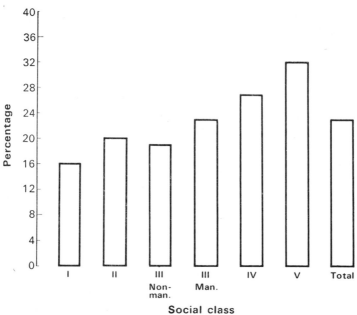

(see Fig. 18). The medical examination included an inspection of teeth. Examining doctors were asked to report the number of teeth decayed, missing or filled (DMF). It is readily admitted that the use of doctors for performing dental examinations will have led to considerable inaccuracy. Moreover, doctors would usually be handicapped by the lack of proper lighting and probes. Bearing these provisos in mind some interesting findings emerged. For the purposes of analysis, children with no teeth reported as being decayed, missing or filled are said to have 'healthy dentition' and those reported as having ten or more DMF teeth have 'poor dental health'. Overall, 12 per cent of children had healthy dentition and 10 per cent had poor dental health.

There was a clear social class trend; healthy dentition was found most often in the children of Social Class I parents (16 per cent), whilst only 11 per cent of the children from Social Class V families had healthy dentition. There was no difference in the results for boys and girls. Poor dental health was found more frequently in the Social Class V children (10 per cent) than in Social Class I children (7 per cent).

Of the regions, Scotland appeared in a particularly unfavourable light; only 6 per cent of the Scottish children had healthy dentition compared, for example, with 19 per cent in the Eastern region of

England. One recalls that Scotland is said to have the highest sweet consumption in the British Isles.

Dental anaesthesia

Dental anaesthesia is becoming an increasingly controversial procedure. This controversy extends beyond the dental profession and centres around the pros and cons of a general as compared with a local anaesthetic, and the safety of general anaesthesia in the conventional upright position. A review of current anxieties about these procedures is to be found in the Dental Anaesthesia Report of the Joint Sub-Committee which the Ministry of Health published in 1967. The 'normal' child is not included in their list of patient-groups for whom general anaesthetic is justified. In the study, however, nearly half (45 per cent) of the children had already had a general anaesthetic by the age of seven years, boys and girls in equal proportions.

Physiotherapy

Physiotherapy is available free of charge to children under the National Health Service on the prescription of a doctor, usually through specialist services. It has been subject to considerable critical evaluation in recent years and its benefits and positive indications are becoming more widely understood. Its widespread use for minor physiological variations of posture has largely been discredited and resources concentrated on those in real need, especially the asthmatics and others with respiratory disorders, where breathing exercises can be of considerable value.

In all, approximately 4 per cent of the children in the study had received physiotherapy.

A social class trend was once more present with Social Class I children (7 per cent) being the most frequent users of the service and Social Class V (3 per cent) the least.

Child guidance clinics

Recent years have seen a growing awareness of the psychological needs of both child and family and the need for prompt skilled help in the treatment of behaviour and learning disorders. *The Health of the School-child 1966–1968* (H.M.S.O., 1969) stresses the uneven geographical distribution of child guidance and child psychiatry services in England and Wales. An eighty-fold variation is quoted in rates of attendance by schoolchildren between different local authorities from a maximum 38 per 1000 in Grimsby to 0·5 per 1000 in Chester. The English average was 8 per 1000.

By the age of seven, 136 out of 14,528 study children had attended such clinics, giving a rate of 9 per 1000 for the sample as a whole. Twice as many boys as girls had attended. Within England the attendance rate varied markedly; for example, it was five times higher in the London and South East region than in the adjacent Southern region. There is no evidence that the *need* for child guidance varies greatly between areas in Britain, and one cannot but attribute most of the marked variation in attendance rates to the local level of concern and provision, and ability to attract staff. Even in the best supplied areas, complaints of excess work load and long delays for appointments are frequent.

Hospital services

It may come as a surprise to the reader to find that as many as 45 per cent of the children had by the age of seven been admitted to stay in hospital at some time. Hospital admission is an expensive procedure. The cost of a night's stay in an 'acute hospital' is at least £8. Greater, however, is the emotional price paid by the individual child. An illness is not an appropriate occasion to introduce separation of the anxious parent and sick child (MacKeith and Apley, 1968).

It is possible to reduce the hospital admission rate for children. Various attempts have been made to achieve this; for example, the paediatric home care scheme initiated at St Mary's Hospital, Paddington, and the domiciliary nursing schemes in Rotherham and Birmingham. These schemes work well. Their cost in terms of staff per number of patients treated may be high in general practice terms, but is a fraction of the cost of hospital admission. There has, however, been no attempt to increase the scope of these schemes which remain pioneer examples of a different approach to children's medicine. A new type of doctor, the 'community paediatrician', has been proposed; he might lead a service drawn from the staff of the district hospital and the large group practice (Neligan and Jackson, 1970).

Accidents

'Accidents account for about a third of all the deaths of school children and comprise the largest single cause of death in this age group. More than half the fatal accidents occurred on the roads' (*The Health of the School Child, 1966–1968*).

The Standing Committee on Accidents in Childhood of the British Paediatric Association reported in 1967:

The cost to the nation of accidents in childhood must be enormous, yet surprisingly little co-ordinated research is being carried out.

There is need for official encouragement of enquiry into the prevention, causation, management and sequelae of accidents. Much of this could be carried on by collaborative research between the regional accident centres, the local centres and the local health authorities. The prevention of accidents in children seems particularly worthwhile.

By 1965, accidents had claimed the lives of sixteen study children. Five deaths were associated with accidental asphyxia, four being before the child's first birthday. A further five were killed by moving vehicles, the youngest of whom was just over four years of age.

A study has been made of the children who suffered serious disability following accidents. We found that ten children had suffered severe scalds, and a further seventeen had deformities following fractures. Four had lost one or more digits. One example of an obviously 'accident prone' child was a boy who had burned his hand on a poker at eighteen months; fallen off a donkey at three, fracturing his collar bone; fallen in the toilet at four, lacerating his scalp; and caught his arm in the washing machine a few months later.

More boys (2·9 per cent) than girls (1·7 per cent) had had hospital treatment following a road accident. A sex difference would seem to be almost inevitable in view of the more active and less conforming behaviour of boys in our society.

The road accident is now the single most common killer of school children. Although road safety campaigns have at least held steady the ratio of accidents to the number of vehicles, the medical profession with its vested interest in health must play a role in accident prevention with the same zeal that has been shown towards disease.

The frequency of accidents occurring at home is shown by the finding that 9 per cent of the study children had been admitted to hospital at some stage for a home accident; more boys (10 per cent) than girls (8 per cent). Other accidents and injuries (sustained neither at home nor on the road) requiring hospital admission were also reported for 9 per cent of the children, again occurring more commonly in boys (11 per cent) than girls (7 per cent).

Finally, a similar sex difference was found for concussion or head injury (boys 3·6 per cent; girls 2·5 per cent).

Tonsillectomy

The most common operation for which hospital admission was required was for removal of the tonsils. (This operation is nearly always combined with adenoidectomy and the two operations will be considered jointly.)

Approximately one-third of all hospital admissions had been for tonsil-lectomy. In all, 16 per cent of the children had had their tonsils removed, equal percentages of boys and girls having had this operation. It may surprise the non-medical reader that tonsillectomy has re-entered the arena of medical controversy; there has been much recent heartsearch-

Figure 19. Tonsillectomy rate by zone and country

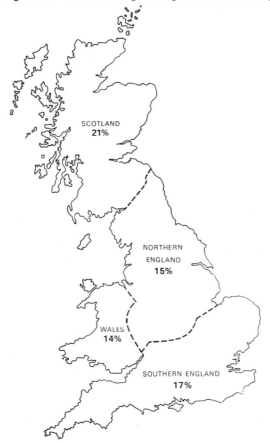

SCOTLAND
21%

NORTHERN
ENGLAND
15%

WALES
14%

SOUTHERN ENGLAND
17%

ing and rethinking as to the need for this operation. In a recent editorial in the medical press, it was stated: 'The fact remains that despite a sprinkling of clinical investigations over the past two years, we know virtually nothing about the value of the tonsils; or how to determine whether they should be removed.' Several recent enquiries have shown that tonsillectomy rates vary enormously even between adjacent and seemingly similar areas.

After allowance for social class differences between the areas, a small difference in tonsillectomy rates was found between the North (15 per cent) and the South (17 per cent) of England; and large differences between Scotland (21 per cent), England (16 per cent) and Wales (14 per cent) (see Fig. 19). These variations are hard to explain. Any of the following considerations could be relevant: a differing need for the operation; a differing demand by parents; a difference in the readiness of surgeons to undertake the operation; and differences in the availability of staff and facilities for the operation.

Analysis of tonsillectomy by social class shows that Social Class III (non-manual) children had most frequently undergone the operation (20 per cent), whilst the lowest proportion was in Social Class V (13 per cent).

Abdominal operation

A total of 234 children, 2 per cent of the boys and 1·2 per cent of the girls, had already had an abdominal operation. Nearly half of these operations were appendicectomy. The earliest appendicectomy operation was performed at the age of eighteen months although in all only twelve had been performed before the age of four years. There are no reported fatalities from appendicitis in the study, but some recent research indicates that the outlook for this condition in childhood is not as good as has commonly been held.

Hernia repair

The operation of hernia repair had been performed on 261 (1·8 per cent) study children. The rate for boys was three times that of girls. The sex difference is due to the more complex anatomy of the male groin. A further 0·8 per cent of the boys and 0·2 per cent of the girls had inguinal hernia present on physical examination, and most of these would be candidates for operation at a later date.

In the introduction to this chapter there was an implied question that perhaps those families who use the services least are the ones in most need. The results leave no doubt that families in Social Class V and to a lesser extent those in Social Class IV make less use of many of the services for children than do other families. It is also clear from the results in this chapter (e.g. on dental health) and elsewhere in the book that the children in these groups tend to be disadvantaged in many ways.

It might be argued that since the services for children are provided, it is up to the parents to make use of them. However, this would ignore the needs of the children. What is urgently needed is more information about *why* certain families do not make use of services.

It may be, for example, that welfare clinics and other services are badly sited for some families. Costly and time-consuming journeys on public transport from out-of-town housing estates to central clinics may be more than many mothers with impatient young children can manage. Clearly, local authorities should consider the availability of public transport, and, not least, its cost, when fixing the location of welfare services and clinics. It is also possible that some mothers find the 'atmosphere' in clinics rather daunting. Certainly, those with large families will often experience practical difficulties. These and other matters, which could be investigated locally at no great expense, could throw some light on this problem of 'differential uptake' of some medical and welfare services.

References

HEALTH AND SOCIAL SECURITY, DEPARTMENT OF (1968) *The Health of the School Child 1966–1968*, H.M.S.O.

HEALTH, MINISTRY OF, (1967) *Dental Anaesthesia:* Report of a joint sub-committee of the Standing Medical and Dental Advisory Committees, H.M.S.O.

MACKEITH, R. and APLEY, J. (1968) *The Child and His Symptoms*, Blackwell.

NELIGAN, G. A. and JACKSON, A. D. M. (1970) 'Paediatric Education in Britain', Chap. 13. in *Modern Trends in Paediatrics*, ed. J. Apley, Butterworth.

7. Development and difficulties

Introduction

A great deal of the information gathered in the study is concerned with development—normal and abnormal. In this chapter we are concerned with some aspects which are conventionally regarded as developmental; the 'milestones' of walking and talking, bowel and bladder control, physical co-ordination and activity level. These are important to consider because failure to achieve normal progress may indicate a need for medical investigation, and in any event is often a source of anxiety to mothers.

In addition the incidence of breast feeding is dealt with. The decline in breast feeding is a matter of concern to many doctors, but the interest in this topic is not wholly medical. As will be shown, there are social class and regional differences in breast feeding, which probably reflect the trend towards what is regarded as normal and acceptable practice in different social groups.

Breast feeding

Until the 1930s the great majority of babies in Britain were breast fed, and it was commonly continued until the infant was about nine months old. The ready availability of safe modifications of cows' milk suitable for infant feeding has subsequently made breast feeding an optional process in the eyes of many mothers and physicians. Douglas (1948) showed that only 45 per cent of babies born in March 1946 were being breast fed at two months of age, although there were marked regional and social class variations.

The results which are presented from our study should be viewed with caution because the information was given by mothers when the children were seven years of age: the mothers' memories may have been faulty, particularly those with large families. Moreover, it should be remembered that the mothers were usually interviewed by health visitors. Health visitors because of their background tend to be identified by the public with the nursing profession. It is therefore possible that some mothers might have biased their answers in the direction which they felt would be more acceptable to the interviewers, particularly if they were not quite sure of the answer. For instance, the reported prevalence of breast feeding after one month may be an overestimate of the actual prevalence. On the other hand information as to whether the children were breast fed *at all* is likely to be more accurate because it does not involve any recall of a time factor.

Nearly one-third of the children were reported never to have been fed at the breast. During the first month of life a further 25 per cent of the children went over to cows' milk. Thus, at the end of one month less than half of the sample (44 per cent) were still being breast fed according to the mothers' reports.

Obvious advantages of breast feeding have long had acceptance: the milk is instantly available; it is of the correct composition for the human infant and has the advantage of being less open to the risk of contamination. The sporadic cases of gastroenteritis seen today occur almost entirely in bottle-fed babies. 'The breast fed infant has always been safe from this serious infection' (Hutchison, 1968).

It is now realised that the composition of cows' milk has certain important disadvantages compared with human milk. The electrolyte content of cows' milk, especially of sodium chloride and phosphates, is higher than in human milk; and cows' milk proteins may cause an antibody response if absorbed from the gut in the first few weeks of life. Risks of artificial feeding, including the incidence and danger of hypo-calcaemic convulsions, and the possible role in 'cot death' of milk antibodies after absorption of cows' milk antigens from the gut have recently been stressed (Stroud, 1969). Professor Stroud concluded: 'Perhaps the time has come for doctors to realise that there are firm, objective reasons for encouraging mothers to breast feed, especially in the first few weeks of life.'

The results from the study showed a strong social class trend in breast feeding. For example, 79 per cent of the Social Class I children had been breast fed initially compared with 64 per cent in Social Class V. By one month the proportion being breast fed in Social Class I had dropped to 59 per cent but in Social Class V it was down to 36 per cent. The possibility of differential bias in reporting in different social classes should not be overlooked, but it is unlikely to account for the observed trend, which confirms that found by Douglas (1948).

What of the national and regional differences? Nearly half of the Scottish children were reported *never* to have been breast fed, compared with 43 per cent in Wales, 32 per cent in the North of England and 25 per cent in the South (see Fig. 20). Analysis showed that these differences could not be explained in terms of social class differences between these areas.

The variation in practice between different occupational groups and different parts of Britain is clearly of interest to the sociologist and the psychologist. Is it linked to the proportions of hospital births in these groups? Or to attendance at antenatal clinics? How does it fit into the general patterns of child rearing? To the extent that medical practitioners are concerned at the decline in breast feeding, the answers have implications for them too. How can they persuade mothers to change their practice? A study of the factors involved and the underlying

Figure 20. Percentage of children who were never breast fed by zone and country

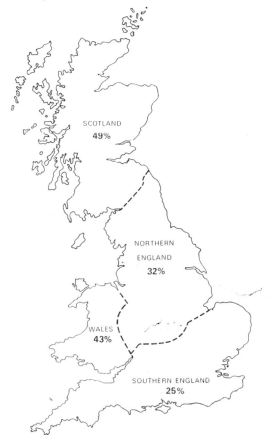

attitudes would be a wise investment in terms of the effectiveness of any medical campaign.

Walking and talking

In recent years there has been much medical study of the developing child. A new subspecialty 'developmental paediatrics' has come into being. Sheridan (1969) has summed up this subject as being 'concerned with maturational processes (from foetal viability to full growth) in the structure and function of *normal* and abnormal children, for three purposes; *first*, to promote optimal physical and mental health for all children, *second*, to ensure early diagnosis and effective treatment of handicapping conditions of body, mind and personality, *third*, to discover the cause and means of preventing such handicapping conditions'.

Two stages of children's development which parents almost invariably await with eagerness are walking and talking. The difficulties of retrospective reporting meant that accurate information about the children's ages when they passed these 'milestones' could not be obtained. Instead it was decided to ask the mothers whether or not their children were 'walking alone' at eighteen months or 'talking' (i.e. joining two words) by two years of age.

It was felt that the mothers would have been concerned if their children had not been walking or talking at these ages and might therefore remember this information with reasonable accuracy, even after five or six years had elapsed. Nevertheless the proportions reported should be viewed with some caution.

The great majority of children can be expected to walk unaided by fifteen months and failure to walk by eighteen months indicates the need at least for medical review. All but 4·3 per cent of the study children were reported to have been walking by eighteen months: more boys (4·9 per cent) were retarded in this respect than girls (3·6 per cent). An analysis of the social class differences supported the observations of Neligan and Prudham (1969) that the lowest proportions of children failing to walk by eighteen months are found towards the middle of the social class scale. Figure 21 shows that whereas amongst skilled manual workers' children (Social Class III manual) only 3·6 per cent had not walked by this stage, the proportions in Social Class I and V were both over 5 per cent. This is a finding which requires further study, since the reasons for it are not clear.

Some 6 per cent of the children were reported as not to have talked by two years of age; and there was a marked sex difference, again in the girls' favour. For this 'milestone', however, there were no very clear social class differences.

Figure 21. Percentage of children not walking by the age of eighteen months by social class

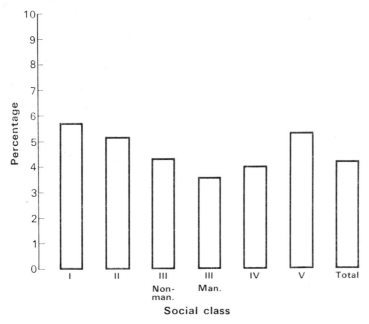

Bladder and bowel control

Retrospective information about the children's attainment of bladder and bowel control was obtained from mothers, who were asked whether the children were 'wet by night after five years of age' and whether they 'soiled by day after four years of age'.

In view of the comments made in the previous two sections about retrospective reporting, it is not necessary to labour the point. Nevertheless, it seems unlikely that the direction of any sex differences would be affected by this, or that social class differences could be wholly explained by differential social class bias in reporting.

Soiling by day after four years of age

This symptom, most upsetting to both parent and child, was reported in slightly over one in a hundred children. It was three times as common in boys (2 per cent) as in girls (0·6 per cent); and it was lowest in Social Class I children (0·5 per cent) with a trend up to Social Class V (1·6 per cent).

It is interesting to speculate whether these reported differences—both sex and social class—are related to different social pressures to be 'clean', to emotional disturbance, or to developmental delay in sphincter control. All three would seem to be tenable theories and further research is needed.

Bed-wetting after the age of five years

'It is understandable that the normal age at which a child may be expected to be dry can only be defined within wide limits. Thus, an intelligent child receiving adequate but not excessive maternal attention will usually acquire diurnal control during the second year, and will cease to wet the bed, except for occasional lapses, during the latter part of the third year' (Ellis and Mitchell, 1968). Ellis continues: 'Persistent enuresis during the day should be regarded as abnormal after the age of three and persistent bed-wetting after the age of four years.'

In recent years parents have more readily sought medical help for their enuretic children. Enuresis has at last become a focus of serious medical interest and the subject of much 'research', not always based on firm scientific principles. Drug treatment remains empirical and subject to pharmaceutical fad, a recent disturbing tendency being the advocacy of powerful antidepressant drugs similar to those used in the treatment of the more severe psychiatric illnesses.

Enuresis is not a disease in itself, but a symptom that points to a need for understanding and some investigation. There is no doubt that notice should be taken of more than occasional bed-wetting after the fifth birthday. Physicians have long abandoned the search for a single cause for this condition and realise that it is often a manifestation of some underlying problem. In a few cases it is a pointer to severe disease, such as recurrent or persistent urinary infection, often secondary to an abnormality of the renal tract. Rarely, it is a manifestation of some underlying endocrine disorder, for example, diabetes mellitus.

Enuresis occurs more often in the mentally retarded than in the intellectually normal child, a reflection of the slow learning pattern. Sometimes the cause may lie entirely in terms of psychiatric upset. There is commonly a return to a more infantile pattern of behaviour and treatment of this behaviour pattern may ameliorate the enuresis.

Dryness is usually achieved during a 'plastic' period of brain development—the critical learning period during the third year. It has been suggested that emotional stress at this time is particularly likely to interfere with the learning of bladder control (MacKeith, 1964). We must remember that any physical disease takes its psychological toll and at times it may be difficult to determine the underlying cause of enuresis; or, indeed, which is cause and which is effect.

The mothers in the study reported that one in nine (11 per cent) of the children were wetting their beds (apart from the occasional mishap) after the age of five; boys were reported to be bed-wetters (12 per cent) more than girls (10 per cent). An analysis of social class differences showed a trend from Social Class I (10 per cent) to Social Class V (14 per cent).

As with the results for soiling, it is interesting to consider the reasons for these differences. Are they related to parental attitudes in different social class groups? Is there less 'pressure' on boys to be dry than on girls? Or is the sex difference a developmental phenomenon?

Information available in the study does not enable us to attempt answers to these questions. On the other hand, preliminary analyses have suggested interesting lines for further work with the study data. For example, the bed-wetters were more often found in large families, and they were more often born to older mothers. However, since mothers with large families will tend at a point in time to be older than mothers with small families, we may be observing the same effect. Alternatively, these associations may be explicable in terms of the observed social class differences. The results also show that the bed-wetters were at the age of seven less well adjusted in school as measured by the Bristol Social Adjustment Guide. However, it has been shown (see p. 33), that poor social adjustment is associated with large family size and low social class, so that the association between bed-wetting at five years and poor adjustment at seven could be explicable in terms of social class or family size or both.

Problems of physical co-ordination and activity level

Considerable interest is now being paid to the problems of children who are clumsy, inco-ordinate or overactive. On the one hand, it seems reasonable to assume that such characteristics as physical co-ordination and activity level are distributed in the population in the same manner as, say, height (i.e. most children are around average; some are above and others below average). On the other hand it is often suggested that at the bottom end of the scale there are a number of children whose poor performance is due to some relatively minor degree of brain damage. However, in general there are usually no other neurological signs in such children.

Whatever the reason for their difficulties, there is no doubt that inco-ordinate children may suffer at school from their lack of proficiency in games and handicrafts. The overactive child will often find difficulty in concentrating upon his schoolwork and may in consequence fail to make satisfactory progress.

Both the teachers and the mothers in the study were asked questions about the children's co-ordination and activity level. In order to distinguish those children whose difficulties were either more extreme or more easily identifiable, the questions described each characteristic and the teacher (or mother) was asked to say whether the description 'certainly applied' or 'applied somewhat'. The results presented are in respect of those who were 'certainly' identified as having the characteristic.

The most marked and consistent findings are the sex differences, which always favoured the girls. For example, 11 per cent of the boys were described by their teachers as 'hardly ever still' compared with 5 per cent of the girls. The mothers described 10 per cent of the boys as 'awkward or clumsy' when 'tying a bow' compared with 4 per cent of the girls. The size of the proportions differed for various characteristics but the boys' proportions were usually about twice those of the girls'.

The social class analyses yielded interesting results. There were consistent social class trends where *fine motor movements* were concerned (i.e. 'awkward or clumsy when tying a bow', 'poor control of hands'); when *activity level* was rated (i.e. 'hardly ever still', 'restless and over-active'); and also for 'clumsiness'. These trends were shown both in ratings by teachers and by mothers and favoured the higher social class groups. For example, the trend on 'poor control of hands' was from 2·6 per cent (Social Class I) to 5·9 per cent (Social Class IV).

On the other hand, when *gross motor movements* were considered there were no such trends as, for example, when the teachers rated 'poor physical co-ordination' and the mothers described awkwardness or clumsiness in walking, in running or in climbing stairs.

It may be that the results which emerged are at least in part related to norms of behaviour and social training in different social groups. For example, middle-class children might at home be expected more often to exercise some restraint on their behaviour ('Sit still at the table' etc.) than working-class children. Middle-class children might also have more opportunities and encouragement than working-class children to draw, paint and tie a bow, and would therefore be more advanced with fine motor movements. But with walking, jumping and throwing the middle-class children would have no such socially conditioned advantages.

These suggestions are purely speculative and there is no way of verifying them with the information from the study. Even if they are valid, they may not wholly account for the differences. There may also be a proportion of children whose inco-ordination or overactivity is caused by 'minimal brain damage'. However, as has been mentioned, confirmatory evidence for such neurological impairment is very difficult to establish. Whatever the *reasons* for the difficulties, the difficulties themselves remain, and may well handicap the affected children in their handwriting, drawing and handwork in school; and the restlessness could mitigate against successful concentration in academic and other work.

Allergic disorders: asthma, eczema and hayfever

Asthma, eczema and hayfever appear to have much in common. The causes are not yet completely understood but they are often reactions to allergic stimuli and sometimes to stress; not infrequently two or all three of the conditions co-exist in the same person, or occur in the family of an affected person.

These three conditions are amongst the most common of the chronic or recurrent ailments. The mothers reported that 3·1 per cent of the children had at some time had one or more attacks of asthma; 5·5 per cent had had hayfever or sneezing attacks; and 5·2 per cent had suffered from eczema even after the first year of life. The medical examinations revealed that 2·5 per cent of the children had visible signs of eczema at the age of seven years. The associations between these conditions were very striking: of the children reported to have had one or more attacks of asthma, 30 per cent had had eczema after the first year of life, 14 per cent still had eczema on examination at seven years, whilst 35 per cent had had hayfever or sneezing attacks.

More boys (3·8 per cent) than girls (2·3 per cent) were reported to have had one or more attacks of asthma; and there was a similar sex difference for hayfever (boys 6·1 per cent; girls 5·0 per cent). On the other hand the history and examination revealed no sex differences for eczema.

Interesting social class and geographical variations were found. The reported prevalence of each of the allergic conditions was greater in children of non-manual than manual class families, being approximately twice as high in Social Class I as in Social Class V. The geographic pattern tended for each condition to reveal a lower prevalence in Scotland and the North of England than in Wales or in the Regions of the South of England. For instance the highest reported rates for asthma were in Wales (5·0 per cent) and in the southern zone of England (3·5 per cent); the lowest were in the northern zone of England (2·7 per cent) and in Scotland (2·3 per cent). This pattern is of course, consistent with the fact that children of non-manual class parents, with a higher prevalence in the South, were more often reported to have suffered from asthma and the other allergic conditions. However, a further analysis carried out in the case of asthmatic children showed that neither the national differences nor the differences between zones of England could be accounted for by the social class differences. Clearly

4

the reasons for the social class gradient and the North/South variation in these allergic disorders merit further investigation.

References

DOUGLAS, J. W. B. (1948) *Maternity in Great Britain*, Oxford University Press.

ELLIS, R. W. B. and MITCHELL, R. G. (1968) *Disease in Infancy and Childhood*, E. & S. Livingstone.

HUTCHISON, J. H. (1968) *Practical Problems in Paediatrics*, Lloyd Luke.

MACKEITH, R. C. (1964) A new concept in development, *Develop. Med. Child. Neurol.*, **6**, 111.

NELIGAN, G. A. and PRUDHAM, D. (1969) 'Norms for four standard developmental milestones by sex, social class and place in family', *Develop. Med. Child. Neurol.*, **11**, 413–22.

SHERIDAN, M. (1969) *Health Trends*, **1**, No. 2, 4–7.

STROUD, C. E. (1969) 'Advances in Paediatrics' *Practitioner*, **203**, 438–43

8. Influences on physical growth

Most of this book is concerned with aspects of children's development or of their environment. Many of the results have practical implications for those who are concerned with trying to prevent or to deal with ill-health, educational backwardness, bad housing conditions, poor social adjustment and so on.

At first sight, the study of children's physical growth does not seem to have the same practical value. It is not without interest, of course, and certain scientists—biologists, physiologists, anthropometricians—will derive important information for their theoretical work. But does the study of growth have any value beyond this? First, it should be said that there is often no very clear distinction between 'theoretical' work and work which has a practical orientation. Often the two approaches feed one another with ideas.

More specifically, a study of the factors which influence children's height may be important in gaining further insight into some aspects of dwarfism or abnormally large stature. Thirdly, height is a very useful indicator of general physical development and its study may give valuable pointers to circumstances before, during or after birth which have an adverse effect upon development. The relative ease and accuracy with which it can be measured is a considerable advantage.

An analysis was carried out to estimate the possible effects of nine different factors on height. It seemed likely that one or more of the factors could explain the effect of another. For example, children in Social Class I and II are taller than children in Social Class V. But is this because mothers in Social Class I and II are taller than mothers in Social Class V?

The following possible influences on height were studied:

Social class
Sex

Birth order (i.e. 'parity')*
Number of younger brothers and sisters
Birthweight
Length of pregnancy
Mothers' age at the birth of the child
Mothers' height
Mothers' smoking during pregnancy.

The analysis made it possible then, to estimate the influence of each
factor upon children's height after allowance had been made for the
effects of all the others. A more detailed description of this has been
reported elsewhere (Goldstein, 1971).

Social class

The first important finding was that the manifest differences in maternal height do not account for the social class differences in children's

* 'Parity' is the number of previous live and stillborn children.

Figure 22. Social and biological factors and children's height

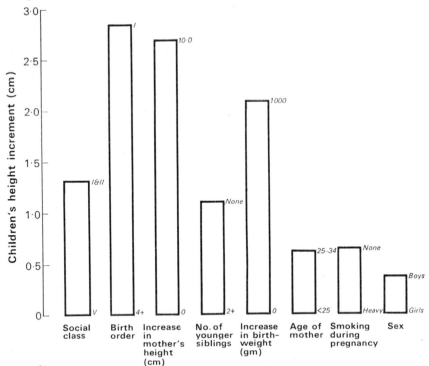

height. In fact, when allowance is made for all the other factors, the effect of social class is approximately halved. Thus, these factors account for only some of the social class variation (see Fig. 22).

There is an overall difference of 3·3 cm (1·3 inches) between children from Social Classes I or II and those from Social Class V. It is interesting to note that this difference agrees quite closely with that found by Douglas (1964) with children of the same age but born twelve years earlier. It seems then that although children are tending to get taller each decade (Tanner, 1962) the gap between the social classes is not narrowing.

Sex

There was a small overall difference in height (0·8 cm) between the boys and the girls; the boys were taller. However, the relationships of the other factors with height were not different for boys and girls, so that separate sex analyses were not necessary.

Birth order and number of younger brothers and sisters (siblings)

It is well established that children from large families tend to be shorter than those from small families. It is also known that later born children tend to be shorter than earlier born children. Needless to say, these two findings are closely related since amongst a group of children of a given age, those of high birth order will also tend to come from large families.

In normal circumstances (i.e. leaving aside stillbirths and deaths) two aspects of family size can be distinguished: the number of siblings born *before* the child in question, which gives the birth order; and the number of siblings born *after* the child (i.e. the younger siblings). In our analysis, these two aspects were kept separate and their effects on height were estimated.

This produced some interesting results. First, for any given number of younger siblings, firstborn children are 2·8 cm taller at seven years of age than fourth or later born children, after allowing for the other factors. *Also*, for a given birth order, those children with no younger siblings are 1·1 cm taller than those with two or more younger siblings.

The effect of birth order on height is *opposite* to its effect on birthweight, where the later born children are heavier (Butler and Alberman, 1969). It is generally accepted that the reason for this increased birthweight is that the intrauterine or prenatal environment is more favourable for later children. It therefore seems that the postnatal environment, shared as it is with older children who are in a sense competing for the same resources, is relatively unfavourable to the later born child. Furthermore,

if younger siblings appear the environment becomes still more unfavourable.

The effect of birth order and younger siblings on height is illustrated
in Fig. 22.

Mother's height

It is a matter of common observation, confirmed by research, that
children's height is related to their parents' height. However, a topic
which has received some attention in recent years is the possibility of a
closer relationship between mother's and daughter's height than
between mother's and son's; and, similarly, for father's and son's etc.
While the results from some relatively small-scale studies have suggested
that this is the case, more recent larger scale investigations (e.g. Tanner,
Goldstein and Whitehouse, 1970) have not confirmed these findings.

The results from our study establish beyond reasonable doubt that at
the age of seven at least, the height of girls shows no closer relationship
with their mothers' height than does the height of boys.

Mother's age

After allowing for the other factors, the children of mothers who were
under twenty-five years at the birth of the child were on average 0·6 cm
smaller than the children of mothers aged twenty-five to thirty-four years.
The reasons for this are not clear, particularly since maternal age does
not seem to affect birthweight after allowance has been made for
relevant factors. The effect, of course, is small and it may reflect social
circumstances or regional differences associated with maternal age for
which allowance has not been made.

Birthweight and length of pregnancy

It is useful to consider these factors together because, of course, they are
closely related. Children born before the 38th week of pregnancy are
lighter in birthweight than those born at term. They were also found to
be on average 1·1 cm shorter at the age of seven years. However, when
allowance was made for all the other factors, there was no relationship
between the length of pregnancy and the children's height. On the
other hand the effect of birthweight remained: there was an average
gain in height at seven years of 2·1 cm for each kilogram of birthweight.

Smoking in pregnancy

Smoking by mothers during pregnancy has been shown to be associated
with increased risk of perinatal death (Butler and Alberman, 1969).

This increased risk can be attributed to the lowered birthweight of babies of mothers who smoke.

In order to investigate the relationship between smoking in pregnancy and children's height we first compared the height at seven of those children whose mothers regularly smoked ten or more cigarettes a day after the fourth month of pregnancy ('heavy smokers'); those children whose mothers smoked 1 to 9 a day ('medium smokers'); and those children whose mothers smoked less than one per day ('non-smokers'). The 'heavy smokers' children were 1·3 cm and the medium smokers' children 0·9 cm shorter than the non-smokers' before allowance was made for other factors.

The question which was then posed was: does the relationship between smoking in pregnancy and lowered birthweight account for the later relationship between smoking in pregnancy and height? The answer is No. When birthweight and all the other factors were taken into account the height differences, although reduced, did not disappear. There remained an average difference of 0·6 cm between the children of the heavy and non-smoking mothers (Fig. 22).

This is further evidence for the damaging effect of smoking in pregnancy, although—as with mothers' age—the residual difference may reflect additional factors which are associated with heavy smoking amongst mothers and perhaps also with a postnatal environment which is unfavourable for physical growth. Further study is needed here.

National variation in height (England, Scotland and Wales)

A separate analysis of the national differences in children's height showed that the English children were on average 0·5 cm taller than the Welsh, who in turn were 0·6 cm taller than the Scottish children. These results confirm earlier findings (e.g. Douglas and Simpson, 1964).

The most likely explanation of these differences is that they reflected national differences in parents' height. The mothers' height was known and although the fathers' height had not been recorded, social class is known to be related to fathers' height. When allowance is made for the mothers' height and social class, there are no remaining national differences in children's stature.

Despite the relatively small individual effects, it is important to note that when the factors are considered jointly the effects may be very large indeed. For example, the average difference in height between children who have the most adverse circumstances (i.e. in Social Class V, fourth born or later with two or more younger siblings, with a 'low' birthweight, a 'short' mother who smoked heavily during pregnancy and was aged under twenty-five years) and those who have the most advantageous circumstances, is estimated to be 13·8 cm or 5½ inches.

One of the most urgent questions which arise is: why is there an effect of smoking in pregnancy on children's height? It has been pointed out that smoking in pregnancy is associated with lowered birthweight, but this does not account for the subsequently smaller stature of children of mothers who smoked during pregnancy. Is there some damage to the baby in the womb which continues to have an effect on the physical development of the growing child? Or can the effect be accounted for by some as yet unexplained aspect of the postnatal environment of children whose mothers smoke?

References

BUTLER, N. R. and ALBERMAN, E. D., eds (1969) *Perinatal Problems*, Livingstone.

DOUGLAS, J. W. B. and SIMPSON, H. (1964) 'Height in relation to puberty, family size and social class', *Millbank Memorial Fund Quarterly*, **42**, 20–35.

GOLDSTEIN, H. (1971) Factors influencing the height of seven-year-old children: results from the National Child Development Study', *Human Biology*, **43**, 92–111.

TANNER, J. M. (1962) *Growth at Adolescence*, Blackwell.

TANNER, J. M., GOLDSTEIN, H. and WHITEHOUSE, R. H. (1970) 'Standards for children's heights at ages 2–9 years based on parents' heights', *Arch. Dis. Childh.*, **45**, 566–69.

9. Vision, speech and hearing

Introduction

The 'special senses' are of vital importance; they are the media through which most interpersonal communication takes place. It follows that impairment of vision, speech or hearing may at best create irritation and inconvenience for a child and at worst may have a crippling effect upon his social adjustment, his schooling and his progress through life. For appropriate and effective action to be taken, early detection is crucial.

Vision

'More children have defective vision than any other defect, excluding dental disease', reported the Chief Medical Officer of the Department of Education and Science in 1966; and he went on to say that, 'failure to make satisfactory progress (in school) is frequently due to undetected visual defect'. It should be added that this is particularly lamentable in view of the relative ease with which visual defects can be detected and corrected.

There is gross variability in the assessment and definition of visual defect in different local authorities; in his biennial report for 1964–65 the Chief Medical Officer described the numbers of children needing treatment or observation as varying from 22 to 358 per thousand and that of squint from one to 14 per thousand. Since the prevalence and types of visual defect vary with age, some of these discrepancies may be explained by the age range of the children examined by school medical officers but this cannot account for all the reported difference. In the present study, where medical officers were asked 'Is there evidence of a squint?' there was no difference in prevalence of squint by region.

An important part of the study's medical examination was the testing of distant vision, using a standard Snellen test chart. Instructions were given about the conditions of the test, as well as on the procedure to be adopted when the child did not know his letters. Each eye was tested separately without glasses, and again with glasses if these were worn. The examining medical officers tested 92 per cent of the study children.

Figure 23. Differences of visual acuity between better eye and other eye

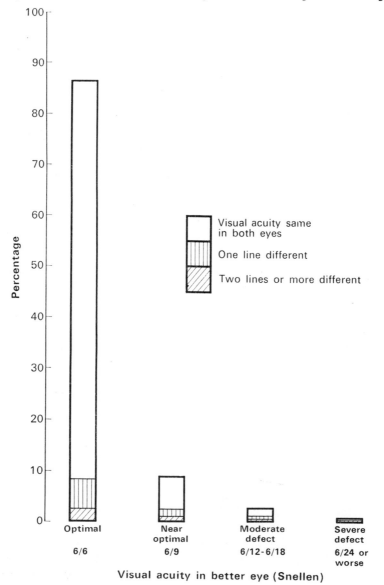

Visual acuity same in both eyes

One line different

Two lines or more different

Percentage

Optimal
6/6

Near optimal
6/9

Moderate defect
6/12-6/18

Severe defect
6/24 or worse

Visual acuity in better eye (Snellen)

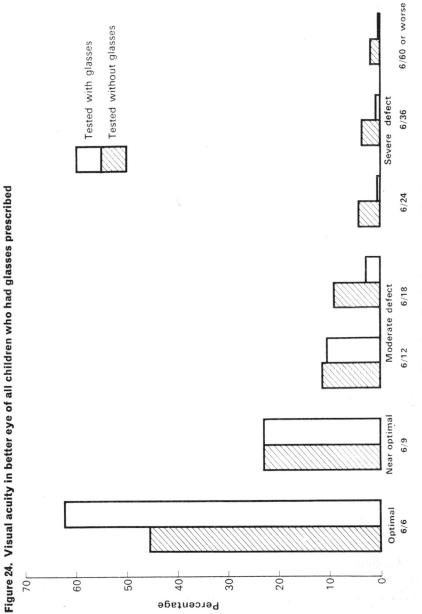

Figure 24. Visual acuity in better eye of all children who had glasses prescribed

In the first report the results were given for each eye separately, and it was shown that 83 per cent of the children had optimal (6/6) visual acuity in their right eye and the same proportion had optimal acuity in their left eye. Fig. 23 shows the acuity of the *better* of the eyes for all children for whom test results were received. It also shows the proportion who could read up to the same line of print size with each eye; and the proportion who had one line difference, or more than one line difference, between their eyes on testing.

In fact some 97 per cent of the children tested had optimal or near-optimal (6/9) vision in their *better eye*; and in all 92 per cent achieved this with *both* eyes. This reassuring finding confirms that the vast majority of children have good vision at the age of seven. What of the remainder? 2·6 per cent had a moderate (6/12 and 6/18), and 0·9 per cent a severe (6/24 or worse) visual defect in their *better* eye. The latter group would have very poor vision indeed without correction. Fig. 24 shows that the wearing of glasses did a good deal to remedy the vision of the children with defects. Nevertheless it should be noted that in the children who have been prescribed glasses (six per cent of the total sample), only 85 per cent of those tested achieved optimal or near-optimal vision in their better eye even after correction. This underlines the recommendation made in the first report, that children wearing glasses should always be put in front of the class if possible, since even after correction a substantial proportion will have suboptimal vision.

Squint

It is well known that there is a strong association between squints and defective vision. The best known association is that of subconscious suppression of vision in the squinting eye to avoid double vision—a defect which may develop into permanent unilateral blindness if not treated in early childhood. It is less commonly known that squints may develop in long-sighted children as a result of a continuous effort to focus on near objects. In other cases it may be part of a generalised muscular inco-ordination involving the eyes as well as other parts of the body; an extreme example is seen in cerebral palsy, where squint is very common. The study of the effects of squints is therefore very complex, but it has been established beyond all doubt that their early treatment can prevent a proportion of visual defects in later life. Indeed it is one of the most positive contributions that preventive medicine can make in this field.

A definite squint (i.e. not 'latent') was one of the commoner physical defects noted in the study, being present in over 3 per cent of the children examined. Fig. 25 shows very clearly the association between

Figure 25. Visual acuity of better eye and difference between the eyes of children with and without squints at seven years

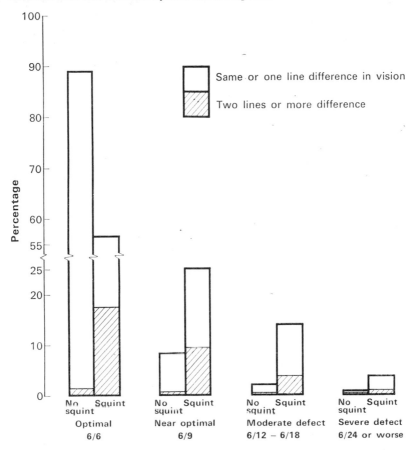

Visual acuity in better eye (Snellen)

poor visual acuity and squints present at seven years. The figure represents the visual acuity of the *better* eye in children with and without squints; and it also shows that in children with squints considerable differences between the acuity of the eyes were very common. These results emphasise a fact well known to ophthalmologists, namely that squinting children tend to have bilateral visual defects, one eye often being much worse. It is a striking finding that of all the children who had been prescribed glasses nearly 60 per cent (557 out of 916) had past or present squints, underlining the importance of the association between squints and defective vision.

An association between physical inco-ordination and squints was also confirmed in the present sample, for the children who were described as 'clumsy' by their teachers were more than twice as liable to have a squint as those not considered to be clumsy. The above results are discussed in more detail by Alberman, Butler and Gardiner (1971).

It has been suggested that squints are more common in children in poor socio-economic circumstances (Miller *et al.*, 1960). Our findings confirm a trend towards the lower social classes in the children with squints. There was, however, no sex difference.

Speech

Difficulties of speech can be a considerable social handicap; they can also lead to educational problems, particularly backwardness in reading (Vernon, 1957). In some children speech problems may be part of a general pattern of retarded or slow development, whilst in others the problems are relatively specific. Emotional stress or maladjustment may be an important factor but one should not overlook the fact that children from families in which the standard of speech is generally poor will lack an adequate model to form a basis for their developing skill.

Only a small minority (1·1 per cent) of the children were reported by the examining medical officer to have a stammer or stutter. However, over 6 per cent of the children were reported by mothers to have had a stammer or stutter at some time during the first seven years. There was a social class trend on the medical examination findings from 0·7 per cent in Social Class I to 1·6 per cent of the children in Social Class V.

It is clear that some kind of speech problem is relatively 'normal' during the first seven years, since one in eleven of the children were reported by mothers to have had 'other speech difficulties' (i.e. other than stammer or stutter). These included a very heterogeneous group of speech problems which are not analysed further here.

A clinical speech test was included in the medical examination. The children were asked to repeat short sentences designed to cover both the letter sounds and most of the combinations of sounds in normal spoken English.

The results showed the expected sex differences, girls making fewer errors than boys. There was also a marked social class trend; the average number of errors rising from Social Class I to Social Class V. One of the most interesting of the regional results was the relatively good performance of the Scottish children on the test. At the least, some substance can be given to the legend that the Scots speak more clearly than the English!

To supplement the speech test, the medical examiner was asked to assess the overall intelligibility of each child's speech on a four-point scale. Some 14 per cent of the children were judged not to have *fully* intelligible speech but in nine out of ten of these children it was reported that 'almost all words were intelligible'.

Teachers were also asked whether the child was 'difficult to understand because of poor speech'. Nearly 11 per cent of the children were reported to fulfil this criterion 'somewhat' and for 2·6 per cent it 'certainly' applied. The findings from both doctors and teachers favoured the girls. There was a social class trend indicating that children in lower social classes are more often lacking in intelligibility.

However, the social class differences here and for the speech test may in part be a reflection of the 'middle-class speech' and standards of most of the doctors and teachers.

The sex differences are consistent with the findings of many others. Do these differences merely reflect some developmental delay in language and speech on the part of boys? Or does our society (and therefore parents) have different standards for boys and girls? Alternatively, does women's speech provide a better model for girls than men's speech does for boys? Or is the girls' better speech a part of their generally more conformist pattern of behaviour?

Speech therapy

There is an acute shortage of speech therapists in Britain. Furthermore, they are very much more thinly spread in some areas than others. Our regional findings for attendance for speech therapy showed up these discrepancies clearly (e.g. 4·1 per cent attending for speech therapy in Scotland but only 1·2 per cent in the North West region of England). However, many published figures show that the variation between individual local authorities is very much more marked than this.

Another disquieting feature of the results was the finding that attendance for speech therapy did not differ between social class groups; the overall figure was 2·5 per cent. If the need is greatest in the lower social classes, why are these children not attending for speech therapy more often? The answer presumably is that parental referral is more often found in the higher occupational groups. Can we consider such a situation as satisfactory?

It is in one sense comforting to find that boys (3·3 per cent) were attending speech therapy more often than girls (1·6 per cent).

Hearing

Hearing impairment is one of the most handicapping of conditions. Severe hearing loss strikes at social competence and often has a crippling effect upon the acquisition of verbal skills upon which much of our education and culture is based. A less severe loss is usually much less debilitating and under good acoustic conditions in a 'face to face' situation may pose few problems even for a child. However normal conditions are seldom good: a noisy classroom, a teacher facing the blackboard, the normal switches of conversation from one person to another. All these situations place a premium on good hearing and even a hearing aid may not fully compensate for auditory impairment. Of course, if the disability goes undetected, the child's problems are increased immeasurably.

One in twelve of the children were found by the examining medical officers to show 'signs of past or present otitis media' (middle ear infection). It is of interest that for one in ten of the children, the doctors gave no opinion. Whilst it is well known that a non-specialist can find it difficult to reach a clinical judgment about the state and health of the eardrum, this is one of the most accessible and important parts of the sensory apparatus.

Nearly 9 per cent of the children had purulent discharge from the ears; the proportions increased from Social Class I (5 per cent) to Social Class V (10 per cent).

Whilst the use of audiometers for the 'screening' of hearing has been a routine procedure in most local authorities in Britain for many years, *clinical* hearing tests have not been so widely used.

The test used in the study was derived from the STYCAR hearing test (Sheridan, 1968). The children were asked to repeat a series of words which were designed to assess auditory acuity over the normal speech frequency range. The test conditions were specified in detail for the examining doctors.

Some 75 per cent of the children were able to repeat all the words perfectly. Girls performed slightly better than boys.

According to the mothers' report, nearly 8 per cent of the children overall had attended a hearing or audiology clinic during their first seven years. Many of these visits would have been for a hearing test following the routine screening procedure carried out in most authorities. There were no sex or social class differences.

Audiometry

The school health services were asked to arrange for the children's hearing to be tested with an audiometer. All but two services could do this. In view of the fact that parents were usually asked to bring their children on a separate occasion for the audiometric testing, the response rate was satisfactory. In all, audiograms were obtained for 73 per cent of the sample.

When a child's hearing is tested with an audiometer, he is asked to listen (through headphones) to a number of sounds (puretones). In the study, his hearing acuity was determined separately for each ear at different sound frequencies ranging from low (250 c.p.s) to high. (8,000 c.p.s.). The level of loudness at which the child can *just* hear at each sound frequency is recorded in *decibels*. If the sound level needs to be raised, say, 40 decibels above an accepted standard level on a particular frequency before a child can hear it, this is conventionally called a 40 decibel hearing *loss* at that frequency.

The audiograms, the results of clinical examinations and the educational assessments were scrutinised individually* for all those children who did not have 'normal' hearing.

Approaching 80 per cent of the children tested proved to have what was regarded as 'normal' hearing, i.e. no recorded hearing loss greater than 20 decibels on any frequency. A further 11 per cent had no loss greater than 30 decibels; and a further 4·5 per cent had a loss of 35 decibels, or worse, but on one frequency only. These last two groups of children had in most instances either a transient hearing loss due to upper respiratory infection or a loss in one ear only without clinical evidence of ear disease.

This left a group of 647 children (5·7 per cent of those tested) who had a hearing loss of 35 decibels or worse, on at least two frequencies. Of these, 473 (4·2 per cent) had a loss in one ear only. Finally, where there was a loss in both ears on one or more frequencies, this was designated 'moderate' in the range of 35 to 50 decibels in 1·3 per cent (143 children); 'serious', 55 to 70 decibels in 0·2 per cent (19 children); and 'severe', 75 decibels or worse in 0·1 per cent (12 children).

Scrutiny of the audiograms revealed a number of general points. First, it was noted that audiometric 'screening' testing on three frequencies only (250, 1,000 and 4,000 c.p.s.) at the 40 decibel level would have picked out all except one of the children with 'moderate', 'serious' or 'severe' hearing impairment.

The other general points relate to the standard of testing as revealed in the audiogram forms. Whilst the great majority were of a high standard, it was disappointing to find that not all of the personnel carrying out the testing appeared to be adequately trained or experienced. At times, the writing and completion of the forms was indistinct; and the symbols used, unusual. Clearly, attention must be given by experi-

* We are indebted to Dr Mary Sheridan for the assessments upon which these results are based.

enced school medical officers or teachers of the deaf to the training of
personnel and the supervision of audiometric testing if the potential of
the audiometer is to be exploited to the full.

Combined analysis of audiograms and clinical hearing test results

Although audiograms were not available for 4,224 children (27 per
cent of the sample), most of these had had a clinical hearing test. *Of
this group*, 2·7 per cent (113 children) were reported to show some loss of
hearing.

Scrutiny of the material (medical and educational) for these 113
children indicated that nine could be regarded as 'partially hearing'
in terms of the categories laid down for special educational treatment;
and two of the children could be regarded as 'severely deaf'. The
remaining 102, whilst needing close educational and audiological
follow-up, were apparently managing satisfactorily in normal classes
without special provision.

In considering the results of the audiometry and the clinical hearing
test together in relation to the likely needs for special educational treatment amongst those children with hearing impairment in the sample,
the following picture emerges:

There were twenty-eight children (nineteen from the audiometric
assessment with a 'serious' loss and nine assessed clinically) who might
be considered to be in need of special educational treatment as 'partially
hearing' children. This is a prevalence of approximately two per 1,000.

A further fourteen children (twelve selected from the audiometric
assessment as having a 'severe' loss and the remaining two on clinical
assessment) on the basis of the evidence available might be considered
to be in need of special educational treatment as 'severely deaf'. This is
a prevalence of approximately one in 1,000.

The implications for teachers of the finding that many children wearing
glasses still have impaired visual acuity has already been mentioned.
The other general implication which emerges is that more research is
needed on the problems of the squinting child. The medical risks in terms
of their visual acuity appear to be fairly well established. However, the
association between squinting and physical inco-ordination suggests
the possibility of educational and other implications.

The chronic shortage of speech therapists has been mentioned, as
well as the local and regional variations in the availability of this service.
When the country faced a severe shortage of teachers, a quota system

was successfully instituted. Should this be considered for speech therapists as a short or medium term measure to ensure that no areas have an overwhelming shortage?

The results from the analysis of the audiograms indicated that all but one of the children with a 'moderate', 'serious', or 'severe' hearing loss could have been selected by audiometric screening on three frequencies only (250, 1,000 and 4,000 c.p.s.). Audiometers which are adequate to this task are available at a very modest cost. If our findings are confirmed, it might be well worth considering the purchase of such instruments for every school; and training school health visitors in the relatively straightforward techniques involved to ensure more frequent and regular auditory screening of children at all ages.

References

ALBERMAN, E. D., BUTLER, N. R. and GARDINER, P. A. (1971) 'Children with squints. A handicapped group?' *The Practitioner*, **206**, 501–506.

EDUCATION AND SCIENCE, MINISTRY OF, (1966) *The Health of the School Child 1964 and 1965*, Report of the Chief Medical Officer of the Department of Education and Science, H.M.S.O.

MILLER, F. J. W., COURT, S. D. M., WALTON, W. S., and KNOX, E. G. (1960), *Growing up in Newcastle upon Tyne; a continuing study of health and illness in young children within their families*, Oxford University Press for the Nuffield Foundation.

SHERIDAN, M. D. (1968) *The STYCAR Hearing Tests;* Manual of Instructions, 2nd Edition. National Foundation for Educational Research.

VERNON, M. D. (1957) *Backwardness in Reading*, Cambridge University Press.

10. Ability and attainment

Introduction

Elsewhere in the book, measures of the children's abilities and attainments are used as 'yardsticks' against which to estimate the effects of environmental, or other, circumstances. In this chapter the relationship between ability and attainment and social class is discussed in some detail together with the need for special educational treatment. Regional differences in ability and attainment are of considerable interest and are considered next. The results show how wide are the variations in educational standards in Britain. Finally, the relationship between reading backwardness and maladjustment is discussed. This is a question which has exercised the minds of teachers and psychologists alike and the results from the study throw further light on it.

Social class differences in attainment and ability

There has been a great deal of discussion in recent years about the relationship between social class and school attainments. This has tended to centre upon the issue of social inequality which, it has been alleged, is reinforced by our educational system.

For example, Douglas's (1964) results indicate that during the years of primary schooling the gap in attainment between children from different occupational groups widens. Although this finding has been subjected to criticism on statistical grounds (e.g. Carter, 1964), there seems little doubt that the phenomenon is a real one. Douglas's later work (Douglas, Ross and Simpson, 1968) suggests that this process is continued in the secondary school.

However, in the discussions and controversies which have followed these and other findings, relatively little thought has been given to the role of the primary school. Attention has tended to centre upon the eleven-plus examination and the selective secondary education which

Figure 26. Percentage of children with below average oral ability (teachers' ratings)

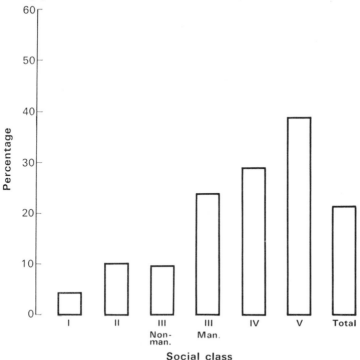

Social class

follows. In particular, the laudable attempts to provide equal educational opportunity for all children have perhaps overlooked the very marked inequalities which exist even before children transfer to junior school. This is partly because very few studies have been concerned with attainments in infant schools or departments, and even fewer have related these attainments to social class.

The relevance of using social class as a measure has been discussed in general terms on pp. 2 to 6. It is not difficult to see why there should be some relationship between a father's occupation and his children's progress at school.

First, heredity is likely to play a part. The relative contributions of heredity and environment to children's abilities and attainments is a difficult question and psychologists, sociologists, geneticists and others will no doubt continue to debate it until we know a great deal more about brain function. However, that heredity plays some part in perhaps setting limits to the rate of intellectual development or to its ultimate peak can hardly be doubted. Since, in general, parents in a competitive

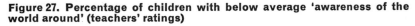

Figure 27. Percentage of children with below average 'awareness of the world around' (teachers' ratings)

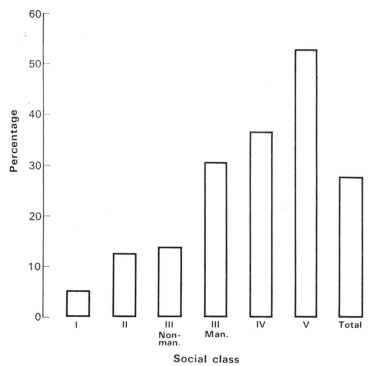

society who have risen to occupations demanding a high level of skill will show a higher level of general intelligence than those in less skilled occupations, it would follow that there will be corresponding differences in their children.

Over and above this, environmental influences will shape a child's abilities and influence his capacity or readiness to learn. A great deal—if not the major part—of learning takes place outside of school and much of this is accomplished even before the child enters school. The vocabulary and concepts used by those around him are vital in providing a framework within which his own intellectual growth can take place. If this framework is bare or impoverished, his own development is likely to be slow; a rich framework of words and ideas will provide the food for more rapid growth. More advanced or abstract thought processes are usually clothed in more elaborate and highly structured language (Bernstein, 1961). A home conducive to learning is one where there is a feeling for the spoken and written word as a tool for conveying

Figure 28. Percentage of children with 'little' or 'no' 'creativity' (teachers' ratings)

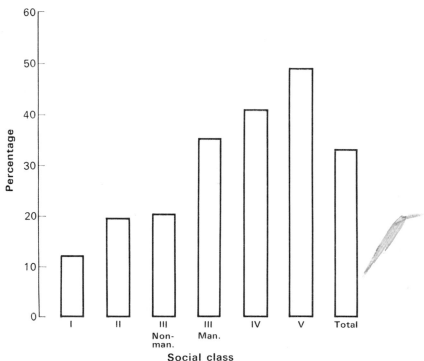

precise meaning; and where children are stimulated to question the world around them and receive explanations appropriate to their age.

There are two senses in which a child from such a home comes to school ready to learn. He is intellectually ready in that his language and concepts are already well structured, so that the school is building upon established foundations. But he is also psychologically ready to acquire new skills. For example, he has learned that reading provides pleasure and he wants to be a part of the literate community as soon as possible. His whole attitude to school is conditioned by his parents' high regard for education.

This kind of home is certainly not a monopoly of professional or other non-manual workers. However, it is more frequently found amongst occupational groups which possess a high level of education and skill. Thus, in examining social class differences, we are examining the effects both of environment and of heredity upon children's abilities and attainments.

Figure 29. Percentage of children with 'poor' copying designs score (0–5)

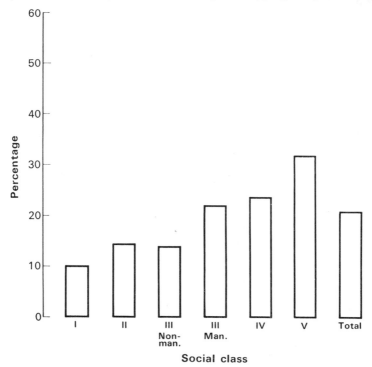

Social class

The results in Figs 26 to 31 show the relationship between poor ability and attainment and social class. The groups of children included are by no means at the extremes. For reading and arithmetic, where test results were available, the children whose results appear in the histograms are those whose score placed them in the bottom 30 per cent of the sample.

Two important points emerge in these two analyses. First, there is clearly a strong association between social class and reading and arithmetic attainment at seven years of age. The chances of an unskilled manual worker's child (Social Class V) being a poor reader are six times greater than those of a professional worker's child (Social Class I). If the criterion of poor reading is made more stringent, the disparity is much larger. Thus, the chances of a Social Class V child being a *non*-reader are fifteen times greater than those of a Social Class I child (see Appendix).

A second point which emerges is that the gradient from Social Class I through to Social Class V is not regular. There are little or no differences

Figure 30. Percentage of children with 'poor' problem arithmetic test score (0–3)

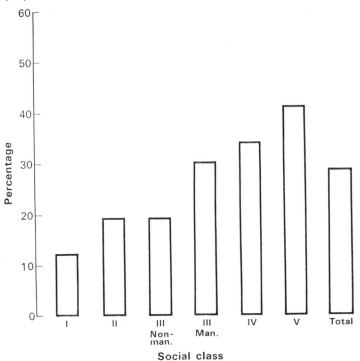

between the results for Social Class II and Social Class III (non-manual) children but very considerable differences between the results of these groups and those for Social Class III (manual) children.

The results for the abilities assessed by teachers' rating and for the copying designs test show the same general pattern with increasing proportions of children with poor ability accompanying lower social class. Again, the gradient of proportions through the social classes is not regular.

It is difficult to draw firm conclusions about the relative differences in the proportions in the social class groups since these are dependent upon the abilities being assessed, the measures used and the stringency of the criteria adopted. However, there appears to be a substantial division between the children from non-manual, or middle-class, homes on the one hand, and those from manual, or working-class, homes on the other. This suggests that whatever the factors are which social class indirectly measures, they are fairly sharply differentiated as between middle-class and working-class homes, at least as far as their effect on attainment or

Figure 31. Percentage of children with 'poor' Southgate reading test score (0–20)

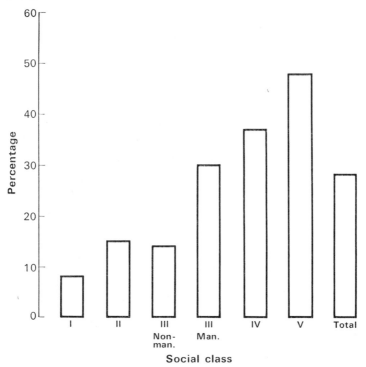

ability is concerned. The results also suggest that there is a meaningful division within the middle-class group between Social Class I children and the others. In the working-class group, the Social Class V children appear to be at a particular disadvantage in respect of poor ability or attainment in school.

Of course, these speculations do not throw light directly on the reasons for the differences. Some of the results in Chapter 4 might suggest that environmental factors are relevant. For example, the proportions of parents who discussed their children with the schools followed the same social class pattern as for the children's abilities and attainments. However, hereditary factors cannot be entirely ignored.

Social class and the need for special educational treatment

The teachers were asked whether the children were receiving any help within the school because of educational or mental backwardness, 'apart from anything which the teacher may be able to do in the normal way'; and, if No, they were asked whether the children would benefit from such help. Five per cent of the children were receiving help and a further 8 per cent were not but would have benefited. The size of this last figure, as was pointed out in the first report (see p. 20), indicates an urgent need to re-examine the provision of special educational treatment in infant schools.

A further question asked of the teachers was whether the children 'would benefit *now* from attendance at a special school'. Some 2 per cent of children fell into this category. The teachers were not asked to choose between special schooling and special educational treatment within the normal school, so that virtually all of the children who would have benefited from special schooling were also said to be in need of help in the normal school.

The results presented in Fig. 32 show the proportions in the social classes. The proportion of children in Social Class V who, it was reported, would have benefited from attendance at a special school was forty-five times larger than the corresponding proportion in Social Class I.

Figure 32. Percentage of children needing special educational treatment by social class

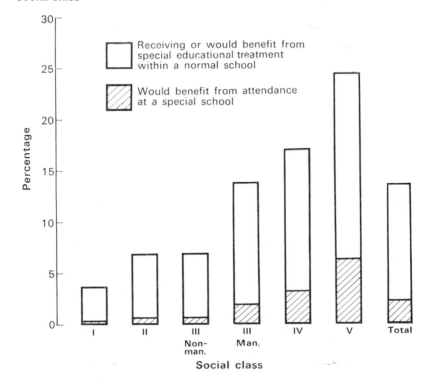

There are two major implications which can be drawn from these and the earlier findings. First, whatever is being measured when social class is used as a variable, it is clearly a very useful predictor. It can be estimated from the above results, for example, that in an infant school of 200 children, where ·100 come from unskilled working-class homes and the balance from skilled and semiskilled working-class homes, some forty children in all are likely to need special educational help within the school on account of backwardness.

Some feel, however, that in preventive terms such remedial action is an attempt to shut the stable door when the horse is at least part-way out. But in the absence of any definitive evidence on the respective contributions of heredity and environment to the social class differences, are we justified in assuming that we can prevent these disparities? Surely the answer is that we have no choice. In the absence of contrary evidence it must be assumed that some form of compensatory education or experience will go some way towards reducing the imbalance. Existing knowledge of child development and learning indicates that the earlier we start the better.

No more than 15 per cent of the children in the study sample attended a nursery school or class and there were very considerable regional variations; although the Government has in recent years relaxed restrictions on nursery school building, facilities still fall far short of the demand or need and will continue to do so for the foreseeable future. Given these circumstances, it is essential, first, to identify those pre-school children in greatest need, and, secondly, to provide the appropriate compensatory experience both pre-school and afterwards. Children from unskilled working class families clearly qualify as a high need group.

Recent experience in the United States has indicated that compensatory experience cannot be provided as readily as one might think. Hopefully, ongoing research both in the United States and in Britain will suggest some leads which will have implications both for nursery and primary education.

Regional and national differences in attainment and ability

The marked social class differences in attainment and ability might lead us to expect that in so far as children from one region were more advanced educationally or more able than children from another region this would be a reflection of the same kind of influences. Therefore we would look for a parallel between the social class distribution for the regions (see p. 8) on the one hand and the children's educational performance on the other. For example, if the south-east corner of England has a higher than average proportion of non-manual or middle-class workers one might expect children from this region to have a higher than average reading score.

However, although the results for the regions do show some overall tendencies of this kind, there are many instances where the regional findings run counter to that expected from the social class structure of the groups. These are of interest for a number of reasons. First, they may reflect genetic factors which are not associated with social class. Secondly, they may throw light upon attitudes in parents and/or children which are relevant to education. Thirdly, they may highlight or prompt an examination of differences in educational practice.

In this context the teachers' ratings of abilities or attainments are of limited value. When an individual teacher is asked whether a child has a 'good background of general knowledge' or, in reading, has 'above average ability' and 'comprehends well what he reads', comparisons with other children are usually either implied or specifically requested. The teachers in the study were asked to rate the individual child 'in relation to all children of this age (i.e. not just his present class or school)' but there are obvious limits to the extent to which the teachers could do this. Most of them would not have teaching experience in more than one or two regions so the standards by which they judged the individual child would tend to be influenced to some extent by the prevailing standards in their area or region. The ratings would therefore reduce any regional differences. For this reason, our investigation here is confined to the results from three tests: the Southgate reading test, the arithmetic test and the copying designs test.

The copying designs test was included amongst the small battery of tests given to the children principally in order to identify those with perceptual or perceptual/motor difficulties. However, all the items in the test are used in intelligence tests and it measures one facet of general ability. Furthermore, it is an aspect of ability which is less likely than most to be affected by environmental influences such as different kinds of schooling, or by parental or community attitudes within our society. Thus one would not expect regional differences other than those which could be predicted from the social class differences between the regions. This expectation appears to be confirmed by the results (Fig. 33). The proportion of children with good copying designs scores ($\geqslant 9$) tended to be highest in those regions with the highest proportion of middle class parents: London and the South East, and the Eastern and the Southern regions. It was lowest in Scotland, which also has the lowest proportion of middle class parents.

However, in reading attainment the most striking feature to emerge

Figure 33. Percentage of children with 'good' copying designs scores by region and country

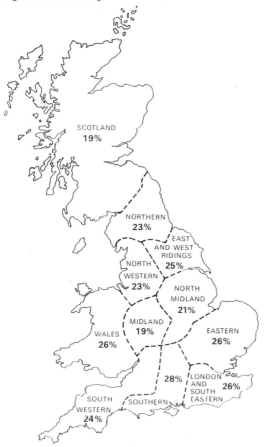

from the results (Fig. 34) is that the proportion of good readers (South-gate reading test score 29–30) in Scotland is markedly higher than in any other region of Britain. This difference is even more marked for poor readers (score 0–20). For example, for every eighteen poor readers in Scotland there were proportionately, twenty-nine poor readers in England and thirty in Wales (see also the analysis on p. 32).

The reading test used was essentially a test of word recognition rather than comprehension. However, the superiority in reading of the Scottish children is also evidenced by the fact that the proportion of children in Scotland who had progressed beyond their basic reading scheme was 10 per cent higher than that in England and 12 per cent higher than that in Wales.

Figure 34. Percentage of 'good' readers by region and country

What is the explanation of these findings? It does not appear that it is directly related to the general educational approach in Scottish schools since, as we shall see, the Scottish children's arithmetic attainment is lower than that of children in many other regions. Three possible explanations suggest themselves. First, Scottish teachers may place more emphasis on the attainment of fluent reading by the age of seven years than do their English or Welsh colleagues; and their educational programme would be geared to this end. Secondly, the approach to the teaching of reading in Scottish schools may be more effective. Thirdly, some features of the environment in Scottish homes may increase the motivation of children to read or advance their readiness to do so.

There is no evidence in the study which might throw light on the first

possibility. However, it does appear that the method of teaching reading
in Scottish schools shows a difference in emphasis from that prevailing
in England and Wales. In Scotland a systematic phonetic—or phonic—
approach is adopted much earlier than in England or Wales. The
implications of this are discussed in detail on p. 133, but it seems possible
that this is at least part of the explanation. It is true that Welsh schools
also introduce phonics much earlier than English schools but without
apparent advantage. On the other hand, a small proportion of Welsh
children at the age of seven would still be having some difficulty with
the English language, so that the Welsh children may not have done
themselves justice on the test, although some of the teachers translated
the test into Welsh to overcome this problem.

Is there any evidence from the interview with parents or elsewhere that
factors in the home might be important in this context? One of the
questions which was asked of the parents was whether they read to their
child. The results show that Scottish parents, both mothers and fathers,
more often read to their children than parents in England or Wales. It is
interesting to note that this is the case, despite the fact that the Scottish
children were already as a group reading fluently. Clearly, then the
Scottish parents were not just reading to their children as a substitute
for the children themselves reading, otherwise one might have seen a
smaller proportion of Scottish parents reading to their children at this
age. This finding supports what must at present be regarded as hearsay
evidence that there is in general in Scotland a higher regard for literacy
than in England.

The results from the arithmetic test (Fig. 35) show a different picture.
Here the Scottish children's results are on a par with children from
England, when allowance is made for social class. Perhaps the most
striking result is the showing of the Welsh children, whose results are
better than English or Scottish, particularly if allowance is made for
social class differences. This cannot be explained in terms of an early
start with formal written arithmetic because the Scottish teachers make
an earlier start than those from any other region without any corresponding advantage for the pupils as revealed in this test.

Do the Welsh teachers place more emphasis upon arithmetic skills
than their colleagues elsewhere? Or are there relevant factors in the
home environment which can account for the findings? At present, these
questions must remain unanswered but in an increasingly technological
society the answers may have important implications.

The results from the copying designs test indicated that where an
ability is likely to be affected by general environmental influences,
regional differences will tend to mirror social-class differences. The fact

Figure 35. Percentage of children with 'good' arithmetic ability by region and country

that regional differences in educational attainment do not follow this pattern must lead us on to look for other explanations. Since the study was not specifically designed to investigate this aspect, our evidence must remain of a somewhat tentative and indirect nature. If the reasons for the differences lie in the kind of emphasis introduced in the classroom, are gains in one direction offset by losses in another? To the extent that differences are a function of community or parental attitudes, it is important to isolate and study these attitudes so that parents can be made aware of their relevance to children's attainments. Finally, further study may indicate that certain teaching methods are more effective than others.

5

However, we must remind ourselves again that the children were only seven years old at the time the tests were given. Future follow-ups might reveal changing patterns of regional or national differences. We may find that regional precocity in attainment is ephemeral or else is achieved at the expense of some other facet of development. Even if this should be the case, it may be a price we would be prepared to pay. Given this knowledge, the choice is ours. Without the knowledge, we proceed by trial and error.

Sex differences in ability, attainment and the need for special educational treatment

The first report of the study (see Chapter 3) examined in detail sex differences in ability, attainment and in the need for special educational treatment for children in English schools. The addition of the results for children in Welsh and Scottish schools and a small number of 'late returns' in England leaves the previous conclusions unaltered. But why do we find these differences? And have they any practical implications?

Most previous studies have shown a sex difference in reading in favour of girls, at least during the early primary school years. In the later primary school years and afterwards the gap narrows and reading skill becomes more complex and more diversified. At these later stages, the particular aspects of reading being assessed (fluency, comprehension, vocabulary, etc.) are likely to influence the relative performance of the sexes differently. However, there is very strong evidence that the proportion of backward readers is higher for boys than for girls at every age.

The reasons for these findings have been the subject of a great deal of debate and discussion which has centred on the question whether, and if so to what extent, the difference between the sexes in reading is related to the capacity to learn to read, or to relevant personality and motivational factors.

The hypothesis that boys' capacity to learn to read is slower to develop is supported by the evidence of the slower development of language skills in boys. In our study, for example, mothers reported more often that boys were late in talking. The incidence of speech difficulties at the age of seven was also higher for boys. Finally, the infant teachers' ratings confirmed that girls have superior oral ability to boys at this age. Additionally, the boys were shown to be more often inco-ordinate or clumsy.

On the other hand, some have argued (e.g. McCarthy, 1953) that the delayed language development in boys is due to the closer contact between girls and their mothers. This, McCarthy felt, gives more opportunity for imitation of correct patterns of speech.

Vernon (1957) stresses the importance of personality and motivation. Amongst the characteristics which she felt to be important in this context were conformity and activity level, the boys tending to be 'less docile and assiduous and less interested in the task'.

The fact that boys are less docile at all ages is hardly in doubt. But why should they be less interested in the task? Perhaps this is because reading is to a large extent a passive occupation, more suited to the female role in our society with which girls will identify.

There is one other aspect which may be relevant and this, too, is related to the roles which boys and girls are expected to fulfil. The male role is less home-centred than the female. Father does more jobs outside the house; going out to work is an essential part of his daily life; and he is more likely to have leisure pursuits which take him away from the home. It seems reasonable therefore to suppose that boys will show more interest in the outside world than girls. Indeed our results confirm that boys at this age are judged by their teachers to have a higher standard of general knowledge, or 'awareness of the world around' than the girls. Some of the early reading material used in schools tends to have no clear link with the world outside the home; the classroom is therefore, perhaps, less attractive to boys. Indeed, some of the most commonly used reading schemes contain material and vocabulary which is not very relevant to the lives of boys *or* girls, particularly working-class boys and girls. In this situation, where the acquisition of reading skill to some extent places a premium upon conformity and desire to please the teacher, it is not surprising if boys make less rapid progress.

It seems likely, therefore, that girls' early advantage in reading is due to a number of factors:

1. Girls' more rapid language development, which may be linked with a faster rate of cortical development, and/or to their closer contact with their mothers, giving more opportunity for developing correct speech patterns as well as more mature language.
2. The generally higher morbidity rate amongst boys which may result in more neurological impairment.
3. Boys' greater interest in 'the world around', whilst early reading material does not always capture this interest.
4. Boys' tendency towards a higher activity level whilst reading tends to be a passive activity.
5. Girls' greater tendency towards conformity which gives them an advantage with material which might not otherwise interest them.

These explanations are consistent with the findings from other studies that the gap between the sexes narrows after the age of nine or ten years.

Thus to the extent that boys are slower to develop language skills one would predict a narrowing of the gap. Also, as reading activities become more diversified and less mechanical as reading skills are mastered, the more active and outward-looking boys would find these personality and motivational characteristics less of an obstacle to further learning. Finally any adverse effects of neurological impairment would be more susceptible to controlling or compensatory mechanisms with increasing maturity.

Why, then, does the gap not disappear completely? Why are there more backward readers amongst boys at all ages? First, perhaps, some of the above difficulties are not resolved for all boys. For example, much reading material for older pupils—particularly for retarded readers—is lacking in interest and thus places a premium on conformity. However, perhaps the most important factor at later stages is the casualty rate directly attributable to early failure, which will necessarily involve more boys than girls. Thus, for example, nearly 7 per cent of the boys were receiving some special educational help compared with only 4 per cent of the girls. A further 10 per cent of the boys were not receiving such help but, in the opinion of their teachers, would have benefited compared with 7 per cent of the girls. In total, therefore, about one in six of the boys was by the age of seven already needing some special help over and above that which their teachers could ordinarily provide.

To what extent are these explanations consistent with the finding that the boys' performance in the *arithmetic* test was superior to the girls'? First, any lag in the development of language would affect arithmetic less than reading. Secondly, arithmetic skills in our society are more closely associated with the male role than the female; boys are therefore likely to be more highly motivated in this area than girls. Thirdly, in most infant and primary schools, number work is more closely linked with activity in the classrooms and increasingly with the 'real world.' outside.

The first implication of the results is that in our society some measure of early retardation in boys' reading is highly likely because of developmental, personality and attitudinal factors. Furthermore, since failure tends to be self-reinforcing, it is essential that those boys who are still finding difficulty with reading at the age of seven, eight or nine are given experience of success in other directions so that they do not lose the desire to succeed or find compensation and self-esteem in undesirable behaviour. When the developmental and other difficulties begin to wane, it is important that reading material appropriate to their age and interests as well as to their reading level is available; and that teachers in the junior school are professionally equipped to tackle the earlier stages of reading.

Perhaps, too, the problems could be somewhat ameliorated in the infant school with an approach to reading which is more active and outward-looking, although this is by no means as easy with reading as in number work.

Much of what has been said above is, of course, relevant to all backward readers, whether boys or girls, but since boys are at much higher risk of backwardness, it is surely prudent to look for ways of meeting their special needs.

Reading backwardness and maladjustment

If a list were made of the possible causes of reading backwardness and, separately, of maladjustment, each would appear as a potential cause of the other. Alternatively, in the individual case, both may be caused by other factors such as unstable home circumstances or brain damage. These situations may be represented schematically:

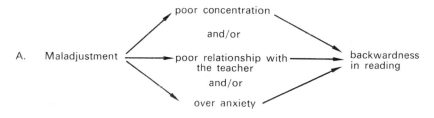

In an *individual* case, the teacher, psychologist or psychiatrist will reach a decision about the possible aetiology in the light of the circumstances of that case. However, it is also important to discover what we can about the relationship between reading backwardness and maladjustment *in general* because this may help in dealing with the individual case. Furthermore, it may enable us to classify or identify groups of children at high risk of backwardness or maladjustment and thus help in the planning of services and programmes of preventive action.

The fact that educational backwardness and maladjustment are often found together is in no doubt; and a number of research workers in Britain have confirmed this (e.g. Burt, 1937, 1946; Chazan, 1963; Pringle, 1965, 1970). What has been in dispute has been the extent and nature of the overlap. Between the wars Burt carried out some large scale investigations in London and Birmingham culminating in his now classic study, *The Backward Child*. Among the causes of educational backwardness listed by Burt were low intelligence, physical ill-health, poor home circumstances, irregular school attendance and a number of 'specialised disabilities'. But he also concluded that in 9 per cent of cases the important factors were 'temperament and emotion'.

In America, Gates (1941) also pointed to the importance of 'personality' in reading disability but arrived at a different estimate, namely, 'that among children with very marked specific reading disability about 75 per cent will show personality maladjustment. Of these, the personality maladjustment is the cause in a quarter of the cases and an accompaniment or result in three-quarters'.

The difference between these two estimates, which may be more apparent than real, highlights some of the difficulties of interpreting and reconciling the results from different studies. Gates was concerned with specific reading disability whilst Burt dealt with general backwardness. It is impossible to know how important were the differences in the criteria of maladjustment and of backwardness. Differences between the social and cultural background of the samples in England and America also make comparisons difficult.

These difficulties of interpretation are to be seen in the many other investigations in this field. Often the groups of children chosen for study are small and unrepresentative. Frequently, there is no attempt to control the age factor, although anyone with relevant classroom experience will know that seven year-old backward readers present a very different picture from fourteen-year-olds, particularly when adjustment is considered. (Sampson, 1966.)

In reviewing this somewhat confusing situation, Sampson suggests a number of lines of enquiry, including:

1. First, the question of the amount of reading backwardness attributable to maladjustment requires careful investigation at different ages and at different I.Q. levels. Studies in different parts of the country would show any local variations in prevalence if the same clearly defined terms and objective measures were used on sufficiently large samples.

2. Secondly, the nature of the maladjustments mainly involved in reading backwardness needs study.

Our study holds out the possibility of tackling all these questions at least within the limitations of the measures used. Furthermore, the long-term nature of the project will make it possible to investigate some of the problems within a longitudinal framework. For example, the second of Sampson's points can be examined in relation to a group of eleven-year-olds, but the kinds of maladjustment associated with reading backwardness at this age are not necessarily the same *even for the same individual* at, say, age seven. Retrospectively gathered information about the situation four years earlier would be virtually useless; an ongoing longitudinal study is the only solution.

These last kinds of analysis in the study must await the availability of material in the second and subsequent follow-ups but there are a number of questions which can be answered now.

First is the question of the amount of reading backwardness which might be attributed to maladjustment at the age of seven. The key issues in such questions, as has already been discussed, are the criteria of reading backwardness and of maladjustment. The Southgate reading test is likely to give much the same results as any other well-standardised test used at this age and the Bristol Social-Adjustment Guide has the advantage that it is readily available and has acceptable reliability and validity. The other aspect of the problem is how selective to make one's group. Are 'backward readers' to be the poorest 5 per cent? Or 10 per cent? On the basis that approximately 13 per cent of the study children were said by their teachers to be in need of some special educational help—most but not all of whom will have been backward readers—'backward readers' for this analysis have been defined as those who scored 12 points or less on the reading test. This amounts to some 12 per cent of the children.

There was a large measure of association between reading ability and adjustment and this is reflected in Table 3. Nearly four out of ten 'backward readers' were 'maladjusted' compared with one in ten of the others.

It is worth noting that if the criterion of backwardness is made more stringent, the proportion of backward readers who are 'maladjusted'

Table 3. Backwardness in reading and maladjustment in school (percentage)

	Stable	Unsettled	Maladjusted	Total
Backward readers	28	35	37	100
Others	69	20	10	100
Total	64	22	14	100

rises. Thus, 54 per cent of the children who were virtually non-readers (score 0 to 3) were 'maladjusted'. This underlines the importance of criteria in this context and makes nonsense of *generalised* statements about the extent of maladjustment amongst backward readers without clear definitions of terminology.

Our results are of particular interest for one major reason apart from the representative nature of the group and its homogeneity with respect to age. The children had been at school long enough for backwardness in reading to be meaningfully assessed but not so long that this backwardness was likely to have led to maladjustment in any but a few cases. Thus the results strongly indicate that in a substantial proportion of backward readers, maladjustment is a cause or an accompaniment of the backwardness rather than a result of it. As we have seen, the degree of overlap is to some extent dependent upon the stringency of the criteria.

It is as well at this point to remind ourselves that the 'maladjustment' being assessed was that revealed in the school situation. If the mothers' reports of the children's behaviour had been used, the results might have revealed a different picture. It is hoped to carry out such an analysis at a later date as well as a more detailed investigation of the kinds of deviant behaviour in school which are most closely associated with backwardness in reading.

It is clear that in trying to help the young backward reader, we should be alert to the possibility that factors unrelated to the specific task of acquiring reading skill may well be responsible for the difficulties. Depending on our criterion of backwardness, it is likely that one-third to a half or more of young backward readers will show severe problems of adjustment in school.

In terms of preventive action and the planning of services, we can regard the presence of adjustment problems in school as a warning signal that reading difficulties will follow in a substantial proportion of cases. The implications of this for the planning of remedial reading services are that these should work closely with psychological and psychiatric services in order to achieve optimal results.

References

BERNSTEIN, B. (1961) 'Social structure, language and learning', *Educ. Research*, **3**, 163–76.

BURT, C. (1937) *The Backward Child*, first edition, University of London Press.

BURT, C. (1946) *The Backward Child*, second edition, University of London Press.

CARTER, C. O. (1964) Review of *The Home and the School*, *Eugenics Rev.*, **56**, no. 2, 93–6.

CHAZAN, M. (1963) 'Maladjustment, attainment and sociometric status', *U. Coll. Ed. J.* p. 4–7.

DOUGLAS, J. W. B. (1964) *The Home and the School*, MacGibbon & Kee.

DOUGLAS, J. W. B., ROSS, J. M. and SIMPSON, H. R. (1968) *All our Future*, Peter Davies.

GATES, A. I. (1941) 'The role of personality maladjustment in reading disability', *J. Genet. Psychol.* **59**, 77–83.

McCARTHY, D. (1953) 'Some possible explanations of sex differences in language development and disorders', *J. Psychol.* **35**, 155.

PRINGLE, M. L. K. (1965) *Deprivation and Education*, Longmans.

PRINGLE, M. L. K. (1970) *Able Misfits*, Longman.

SAMPSON, O. C. (1966) 'Reading and adjustment—a review of the literature', *Education Research*, **3**, 184–90.

VERNON, M. D. (1957) *Backwardness in Reading*, Cambridge University Press.

11. The schools

Introduction

In the last chapter the relevance of the home environment to children's development and educational progress was considered. But what of the school's influence?

It is certain that a great deal of learning takes place before children even reach school; and even during the school years, their experience of the world around them continues to be moulded and extended by circumstances, contacts and media which are outside the school's control. At the same time, quite a large part of children's waking hours during their formative years is spent within the school's ambit. A substantial proportion of our national expenditure is devoted to education in the belief that the extent and quality of the provision is important not only in determining the efficiency of our work force but also in influencing the quality of the nation's life and in helping to establish the kind of community we wish to see. Apart from these long-term goals, the enrichment of children's experience and the engagement of their interest are seen as desirable and important ends in themselves. Finally, there is a growing tendency for parents and schools to see their roles as complementary and to search for ways of making this partnership a closer one.

Any attempt to judge the extent to which educational goals are being realised is bound to be a difficult exercise. In the first place, educational influences are not operating alone and the problems of separating out the special contribution of education are considerable. Secondly, our aims are sometimes such that evaluation is virtually impossible. How, for example, does one attempt to assess the quality of a nation's life? Thirdly, there are no ready means of monitoring the long-term effects of educational policy and practice when children have completed their education.

If these difficulties can be overcome, it is important to define the educational conditions or methods which it is hoped will favour the realisation of our aims. It is of little value to speak in terms of 'good' schools. Whilst most parents—and every educationalist—can to their own satisfaction identify a 'good' school and a 'poor' one, agreement would be far from universal because of differences in the criteria adopted. However, it might be claimed that in any event the most important criteria are so subtle that attempts to measure them are doomed to failure. It is certainly true that in the present state of our knowledge, attempts to assess, say, the quality of the relationships between teachers and pupils would be crude. In a large-scale survey it is impracticable.

However, it is possible to investigate the effects of those aspects of education which present the educationalist with a choice and which can be readily measured. We have recorded, for example, details of the type and size of school attended and the size of class; we know which of the children attended nursery schools and which children have changed schools frequently; we have identified those children who had an early introduction to phonics and their reading programme (see p. 133); and we have made an evaluation of the effects of different lengths of schooling (see first report, p. 24).

At the present stage in the study, of course, the investigation of long-term effects cannot be tackled but for most of the children the end of the school year 1964–65, when the first follow-up was mounted, marked the completion of one phase of their education. Some effects might be seen at their most marked at this stage; further follow-up should reveal the extent to which they persist.

In this chapter we examine first the relationship between class size and children's performance in school and then look at the attainment and adjustment of the children in independent (or non-maintained) schools. Some regional differences in the age at which phonics are introduced, already detailed in the first report, are discussed in relation to differences in reading attainment. And finally, the contacts between schools and parents are examined.

Size of class and educational attainment and adjustment

A reduction in the average size of school classes and the abolition of oversize classes has long been an aim in British education. The Department of Education and Science in 1969 recommended a maximum size of thirty-five for primary school classes. The picture revealed in Table 4 shows how far away that goal still was in 1965.

Table 4. Percentage of study children in oversize classes in England, Scotland and Wales

	England	Scotland	Wales	Total
Classes of 36 or more	61	53	31	58

It should be noted that these figures are not directly comparable with most published statistics, which show the number of oversize *classes*. The proportion of oversize classes is always smaller than the proportion of children in such classes, since the larger classes contain more children per class than smaller ones.

The educational arguments in favour of smaller classes are very convincing. Perhaps the most compelling is that the smaller class permits more individual attention to the children. At the simplest level, the infant class teacher can hear the children read more often if she has fewer of them.

In addition to this individual attention, the smaller class permits a more flexible approach by the teacher; the children's movements about the classroom are unhampered by crowded conditions; desks can be more readily grouped and ungrouped for different activities; and children can more easily discuss their work with other children without the level of noise becoming excessive. It was recently reported by a teachers' association that many infant headteachers felt that large classes made it difficult to achieve a satisfactory level of reading skill before children transferred to junior classes.

The hypothesis might be posed that the smaller class improves the quality of the education given, that it permits more rapid progress in the basic skills of reading and mathematics and that children in smaller classes will be happier and better adjusted in school.

Surprisingly little work has been carried out in Britain to test this kind of hypothesis (Fleming, 1959). Of course, it would be far from easy to make any assessment of the 'quality of education' but educational attainments are readily measurable. Perhaps the outcome has appeared so self-evident that it hardly seemed worth time and effort involved.

In fact, the work which has been done on this question has shown that children in larger classes tend to have *higher* educational attainment than those in smaller classes (Kemp, 1955; Wiseman, 1964; Morris, 1966). At first sight these findings appear absurd; they contradict a common-sense view. Indeed, both Morris and Wiseman pointed out that the results were probably spurious. In the first place, large classes tend to be found in large schools and children in large schools in general have higher attainment for a number of reasons. Furthermore, as Morris explained, poor readers are often placed in smaller classes so that more individual attention can be given. However, none of these workers was able to make allowance for these other factors and show that, other things being equal, smaller classes are associated with higher attainment.

'Other things being equal' is a phrase which trips readily off the tongue but is notoriously difficult to reproduce. However, in this study it was possible to make allowance for most of the factors which might be 'contaminating' the analysis. These were as follows:

1. School size: the relationship between class size and school size has already been mentioned.
2. Streaming: again, it has been mentioned that some schools will group or stream their children in classes so that the less able children will be together in a class, the size of which will be kept relatively small. This is less likely to be a major factor in infant schools or infant classes where streaming in classes is uncommon.
3. Length of schooling: it has been shown in the first report (see p. 24) that children who have spent a longer time in school have higher attainments at the age of seven. It may be that schools which take children 'early' (before five) have larger classes as a result.
4. Independent schooling: children in independent schools are in smaller classes and also have higher attainment (see p. 129) but this may be for reasons other than—or in addition to—the size of their classes.
5. Nursery schooling: children who attended a nursery school might be more advanced educationally at the age of seven. It is also possible that these children might find their way into schools with large classes if there were a heavy demand from parents for places in schools with nursery classes.
6. Social class: middle-class parents are in general more selective about the schools their children attend than working-class parents. Thus if a school has a reputation locally for having high standards, there is likely to be a heavy demand for places from middle-class parents. Such schools would tend to have few, if any, unfilled places and their classes would be relatively large.
7. Interested parents: middle-class parents have no monopoly of concern for their children's education and the children of interested parents, whatever their social class, tend to do better in school than other children. If, then, such parents also try to place their children in schools with high academic standards, which for this reason have large classes,

there might be a spurious relationship between size of class and educational performance.

8. Scottish children: although in general it appears that children in Scottish schools at the age of seven are less often in classes of more than 35 than their peers in England, the preliminary results indicated that rather more Scottish children might be found in *very* large classes (over 45). The Scottish children were also found to be markedly better readers than children in England and Wales.

9. Infant schools and infant departments: although no comparisons have been made between the attainments of children in infant schools and those in infant departments of junior schools, it seems at least possible that there might be differences. There might also be differences in class size between these two types of school.

This then is a complex situation. In any attempt to compare the attainments and adjustment of children in classes of different size, other things are by no means equal!

The procedure adopted to meet this situation was, first, to exclude certain groups of children from the analysis: children in independent schools, children in streamed classes (or in special schools for the handicapped), those who had attended nursery schools or classes and those who were in Scottish schools. Secondly, the analysis was designed to allow for the effect of the other extraneous factors mentioned: size of school, length of schooling, social class and parental interest. Allowance was also made for sex, since although it was considered most unlikely that boys would in general be in larger or smaller classes than girls, it might be that there is a sex difference in response to class size. Finally, separate analyses were carried out for children in infant schools and those in infant departments of junior with infant schools.

The children were allocated to groups according to class size: 'small classes' (30 or less); 'medium-sized classes' (31–40); and 'large classes' (41 or more). Similarly, four school groups were made: 100 or less, 101 to 200; 201 to 260; and more than 260.

Three measures were selected for the analyses: the Southgate reading test score; the problem arithmetic test score; and the Bristol Social-Adjustment Guide score. What were the results?

In none of the analyses carried out did the children in 'small' or 'medium-sized' classes prove to have higher attainments than the children in 'large' classes. On the contrary, the reverse was sometimes the case.

For the children in infant departments of junior with infant schools there were no differences between the class size groups on any of the measures used.

For the children in infant schools, class size was not related to social adjustment. However, in terms of reading and arithmetic attainments, the children in 'large' classes did best and those in 'small' classes did worst. The results of the analysis of reading attainment for these children are shown in Fig. 36.

Figure 36. Size of class and reading attainment in infant schools

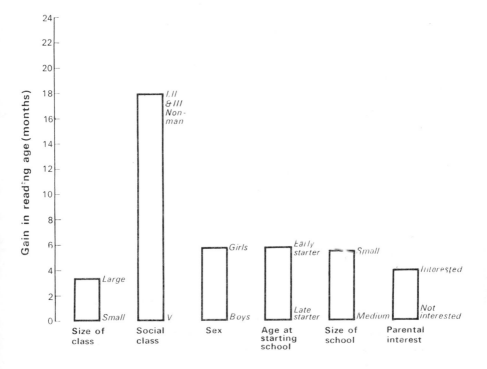

The first point that should be noted about the results shown in the figure is that the effect of class size is relatively small when compared with that of any of the other variables used. For example, the difference in attainment between those in 'large' and those in 'small' classes is only half as big as the difference between boys and girls or between those children who started school before five and those who started after five years of age.

As has already been mentioned, when using this kind of analysis the differences expressed in gain in reading age should be viewed with some caution. They are to some extent dependent upon the class size groupings selected and upon the number and nature of the other variables used (school size, social class, etc.) However, the reading age scale does give some indication of the order of magnitude involved and it will be seen that the children in 'large' classes are approximately three months advanced in reading when compared with those in 'small' classes.

The results are certainly puzzling. Children in small classes do not appear necessarily to derive benefit from their fortunate situation in terms of their attainments in the basic subjects. What is the explanation?

First, it is as well to be clear that these analyses have been concerned with average differences. Therefore the results do not show that all children in smaller classes have poorer attainment. A second reservation is that small classes defined (30 children or less), may not have been small enough for beneficial effects to be apparent. Perhaps classes with less than, say, 20 or 25 children are needed before the advantages of more individual attention are translated into improved attainment. However, the possibility of a reduction in the average class size to 20 or 25 would need a considerable increase in the educational budget and may well be impracticable.

Two explanations of the results suggest themselves, although both are speculative. Neither would seem to account for the fact that class size differences in attainment were found amongst the children in infant schools but not for those in junior with infant schools. This could be due to sampling fluctuations. *However, none of the analyses indicate higher attainment or better adjustment in smaller classes.*

The first explanation is that larger classes might in general be located in urban schools and some research has indicated that urban children tend to perform rather better than rural children in standardised tests. On the other hand, the previous work by Kemp (1955) and by Wiseman (1964) was done in urban areas and an association between larger classes and higher attainment was found.

The other possible explanation is that a large class tends to impose a relatively formal teaching approach and that this may in general be associated with higher levels of measured attainment at the age of seven. A smaller class not only permits more individual attention but, as has been pointed out, lends itself more readily to a flexible, informal, working day. With increasing numbers in the class it becomes more likely that the teacher will find it necessary to impose a more highly structured programme.

It may be true that in general and within certain limits the more highly structured (i.e. the more formal) the learning situation the higher the measured attainment, although it is fair to add that such research as has been done (e.g. Morris, 1966) has not established this. Alternatively, it may be true that a more informal teaching approach is associated with higher attainments only when the teacher is experienced enough to ensure that every child is fully extended. In either case, we should find in examining large numbers of children that the drawbacks of larger classes were offset by the 'efficiency' of a highly structured classroom environment in terms of the children's measured attainment.

These speculations, of course, open the door to controversial issues which are beyond the scope of the present discussion. It should be said, however, that few educationalists would *equate* higher measured attainments with better education, although many would hope that the former would flow from the latter.

The association between *school size* and attainment in the analysis represented in Fig. 36 will not have escaped notice. It shows that the reading attainment of the children in small infant schools (100 or less) was best and that of the children in medium-sized infant schools (101 to 260) was worst. For arithmetic attainment, the children in the small infant schools again did best but those in the large infant schools (more than 260) did worst. For children in infant departments there were no differences due to school size but the size taken here was that of the whole school (i.e. including the junior department). These results are difficult to interpret but in any event are peripheral to the main purposes of the analysis. However, further research in this area would be of interest and may well have policy implications.

It would be unfortunate if the results were to be seen as undermining the drive towards better staff/pupil ratios. At the same time it seems clear that a general reduction in class size at least in infant schools would not necessarily be followed by higher measured attainments, as is sometimes suggested.

If the teaching approach imposed by larger classes is in any sense more effective, perhaps this has implications for teaching in classes of any size. Or is this effectiveness bought at the price of the children's all-round educational development?

Of course the evidence presented here and elsewhere that larger classes are associated with higher attainment may be rejected on the grounds that due allowance has not been made for some important factors in the analyses. However, it is difficult to see what these could be. Furthermore, there is no shred of evidence at present that smaller classes lead to higher attainment—except in the rather special circumstances of remedial classes. Whilst high measured attainment cannot be equated with good education, it would seem wise to spend a very small fraction of the money needed to reduce class size on some investigation of the benefits which should result.

Independent schooling

Although primary education has in general been provided free since 1891 in England and Wales and much earlier in Scotland, independent schools have continued to provide a service for a small minority of children and parents.

Approximately 3 per cent (479) of our sample were in independent (i.e. non-maintained) schools at the age of seven, excluding those who were in special schools for handicapped children. What was their background? And how well were they progressing at school?

The vast majority of the children (442) were in English schools compared with only 16 in Wales and 21 in Scotland. The proportion of the children from middle-class homes (75 per cent) was about two and a half times greater than that in the sample as a whole.

From knowledge of the relationship between social class and other characteristics of the family, one would expect to find some marked differences between the parents of independent school children and other parents. Even when allowance was made for the social class difference, independent school parents were, for example, judged by the schools to be more interested in their children's education than were the parents of the children in local authority schools. The parents were also more likely to have discussed their children's progress with the school. In addition, the mothers of independent school children read books more often and there was evidence that they more often read to their children; and this despite the fact that the great majority of their children were reading quite fluently. Eight out of ten of the middle-class independent school fathers had stayed at school beyond the statutory school leaving age, whereas only a half of the middle-class fathers with children in local authority schools had done so.

On the other hand the stated educational aspirations of the independent school parents for their children were not different from other parents. There were two interesting differences where there was a contrast between the middle-class and the working-class father whose children attended independent schools. Whereas the middle-class fathers took their children on outings or read to them less often than other middle-class fathers, the working-class fathers did these things more often than their peers with children in local authority schools. Does this indicate that middle-class independent school fathers have rather less time to spend with their children?

The independent school children themselves had much higher attainments than their peers in local authority schools. The preponderance of middle-class children in the independent school group would, of course,

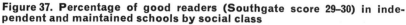

Figure 37. Percentage of good readers (Southgate score 29–30) in independent and maintained schools by social class

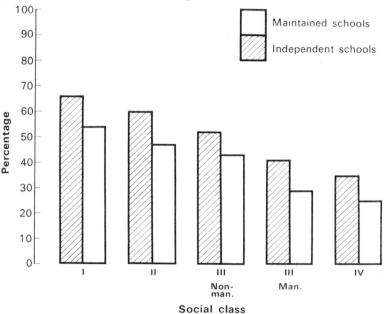

lead us to expect such a difference but Figs 37 and 38 show that this difference persists within social class groups.

However, it may well be argued that the occupation of the father is a relatively crude discriminator and does not adequately reflect the influences in the home. It was therefore decided to carry out another analysis which would make allowances not only for social class but also for the fathers' education. It has already been mentioned that many more of the independent school fathers stayed on at school beyond the statutory school leaving age and it seems reasonable to assume that this would be reflected in a number of other factors. For example, their wives would more likely have received some higher education. Perhaps, too, the general atmosphere in their homes would be more stimulating intellectually. Apart from any environmental influences, it seems likely that children from such homes would have some inherited advantages. The precise contribution of heredity in this context is arguable but it seems reasonable to assume that fathers who were academically successful at school would—other things being equal—have children who show more academic aptitude than fathers who did not have this academic success.

The analysis, which made allowance for social class and the father's

Figure 38. Percentage of children with 'good' arithmetic ability (problem arithmetic test score 7–10) in independent and maintained schools by social class

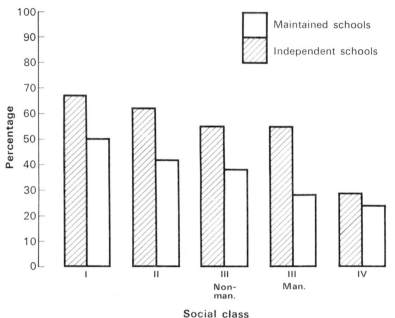

education, reduced the size of the differences in attainment between the independent school children and those in local authority schools, but the differences remained. The residual difference in arithmetic attainment was nearly twice as large as the difference attributable to fathers' education and was approximately equal to six months progress in arithmetic in the context of this analysis. The residual difference between the groups in reading attainment was only a little over half as large as the difference attributable to fathers' education and represented about four months progress in reading. There was no difference between the groups in social adjustment at school.

How should we interpret these findings? No doubt some would wish to claim that the parents of independent school children are paying for a better education for their children and are clearly getting it. Others might see the results as proof that independent schooling even by the age of seven is reinforcing the inequalities in our society. Both views would be premature.

What can be said is that children in independent schools have much higher attainments at seven years than children in local authority schools. Most of this academic superiority can be explained in terms of social class differences between the two groups of children and certain differences in their father's education. But not all. The question which remains is how much of the remaining difference in attainment can be attributed to the children's schooling.

Here we must at present be speculative. It is virtually certain that some of this remaining difference can be explained in terms of factors in the home. Some of these factors, such as parental interest, we have assessed but not yet included in the analyses. Others, such as family income, have not been assessed at all. The relevance of some of these other factors may not be confined to their environmental effect. It is certain that we have not been able fully to take account of hereditary influences. For example, within each social class some fathers will be more successful in their careers than others. In general these more successful parents will command higher incomes and they will also in general—it seems reasonable to assume—be more intelligent. To the extent that the decision to send one's children to independent schools depends on income, the more intelligent fathers within each social class will be able to take this decision. Within social class groups, independent school children may therefore tend to have higher innate ability; they would also have the environmental stimulus of an intelligent father. In the analysis, as was explained, the inclusion of fathers' education as a variable was designed to take account of these elements but it is most unlikely to have done this fully.

The best guess on available evidence is that if all other relevant factors were taken into account, the differences between independent school children's attainments in reading and arithmetic and the attainments of children in local authorities schools would be marginal, with probably a slight advantage to the former. It is doubtful whether any such advantage in measured attainment could justify the additional costs involved for parents. However, we have been looking at the children's attainments after only two years of schooling. The second follow-up, or subsequent ones, may show a different picture. Furthermore, we should remind ourselves that we have been assessing school attainments and not education. It may well be that in a wider educational context independent schooling and local authority schooling each offer particular advantages. The priority which individual parents place upon such advantages will depend upon their way of life, their attitudes to their children and their view of society.

Beginning reading

There is a wide variety of possible approaches to the introduction and subsequent teaching of reading. Some of these approaches differ not in the method used, as such, but in the *media*. For example, perhaps the most widely used innovation in teaching reading in recent years has been the initial teaching alphabet* (Downing, 1964). Here, a simplified but extended alphabet is used but the method of teaching reading need not change.

The methods used in teaching reading can be divided into two major groups: where the emphasis is on the immediate recognition of whole words, phrases or sentences; and where the synthesis of words from their constituent letters or sounds is stressed. This latter group is probably most familiar to parents since they themselves are likely to have been taught to read in this way. The recognition and synthesis of sounds to form words is usually called a phonic approach and the sight recognition of whole words is often called 'look-and-say'. The mature reader normally uses a 'look-and-say' approach when reading but adopts a phonic strategy when tackling a long or unfamiliar word. Clearly, then, the accomplished reader must be able to utilise both strategies, as appropriate.

The argument begins when one comes to consider the strategy which children should be taught to adopt in the first year or two of their reading programme. There are now few, if any, teachers who would maintain that a purely phonic approach should be adopted from the outset, since this is likely to inhibit fluent reading. However, some teachers maintain that children should be introduced to phonics at an early stage so that they can begin to tackle new words themselves. Delaying the introduction of phonics, they maintain, may encourage too heavy a reliance on sight recognition and may encourage a habit of guessing at unfamiliar words. Other teachers feel that the introduction of phonics at an early stage may inhibit fluency; in any event, most children, they say, are not mature enough perceptually until the age of six or seven years to be able readily to recognise the shapes and sounds of individual letters. Far better, they feel, to delay this stage until the second or third year in school when the children will then accomplish quickly what earlier would have been at best laboured and at worst confusing for them.

On the whole, psychologists have tended to support this second view. For example, Vernon (1957) in reviewing the experimental evidence concluded that 'the amount of detailed and systematic phonetic (i.e. phonic) analysis of which children of mental ages under about seven are capable is small'. Morris (1959) reached a similar conclusion: 'As yet there is some divergence of opinion as to the most suitable age at which phonic instruction should be introduced but such evidence as

---

* Information about the use of the initial teaching alphabet and other reading media is recorded on the educational schedules but has not as yet been coded.

exists suggests a mental age of at least six years six months to seven years'. Chall (1967) re-examined this evidence and in particular made a swingeing attack on the most frequently quoted piece of research, that by Morphett and Washburne (1931). She concluded that this and other similar work was misleading and instead claimed that the balance of evidence indicated an early introduction to phonics.

The centre of the controversy, therefore, is the question whether or not most children are mature enough at the age of five or six to adopt a phonic approach to reading, and whether there are advantages in this.

There are two aspects of our results which, albeit indirectly, throw some light on this question. First is the finding detailed in the first report (p. 21) that about 65 per cent of the children had had some systematic phonic instruction *before the age of six*. This is likely to be a minimum figure. The question was a retrospective one and there is a known tendency for people to move their answers to such questions in the 'approved' direction. And the weight of 'informed' educational opinion at present tends to be in favour of delaying the introduction of phonics.

Had the many thousands of teachers involved been wasting their time in teaching phonics so early? Or, worse, had they been confusing many of the children? We cannot be absolutely sure about this and unfortunately we cannot at this stage usefully investigate further by comparing the reading performance of this group of children with the others because it might contain a disproportionate number of able children who were introduced to phonics early because of their high ability. The results from the second follow-up at eleven years, when it was possible to include an intelligence test, should make possible an analysis which makes allowance for ability.

However, there is another piece of evidence which may be relevant here. In Chapter 10 (see p. 109) it was noted that the reading attainment of the Scottish children was markedly better than that of their English or Welsh peers. We also found that an early introduction to phonics was very much the rule in Scottish primary schools. Nearly 95 per cent of the Scottish children commenced phonics before the age of six.

Some of the possible reasons for the Scottish children's precocity in reading have already been discussed and it would be wrong to attribute this solely to early phonic analysis. One contra-indication is that the Welsh children were also introduced to phonics earlier than the English without apparent advantage. However, it seems unlikely that this practice had any deleterious effect.

The study then, provides no evidence that an early start with phonics is advantageous. However, the argument that it is disadvantageous because the majority of children are not mature enough at five or six years is difficult to sustain in the light of our results.

Any comparison of teaching methods is notoriously difficult to mount because of the problems of controlling for the quality of teaching and the motivation of the experimental groups. Such evidence as there is on reading methods strongly suggests that in general the confidence of the teacher in her method, her ability to use it effectively and her relationship with the pupils are more important than the method itself.

Our results indicate that any teacher giving early phonic instruction or any teacher who feels that such a method would best suit her own general teaching approach need not feel inhibited that this would be wasteful of time or counterproductive.

Contacts between schools and parents

'I don't think that any system of education which in fact has to enlist the co-operation and the sympathy of parents can possibly exist without the parents being in the classrooms working alongisde the teachers and the children.' This statement was by a primary school head-teacher, made in a 1969 BBC television documentary programme. Within a few weeks of that programme a head-teacher at a national conference was reported to have described the movement for stronger links between homes and schools as 'a potential Frankenstein monster, which could end with teachers losing control of their schools'.

These views are clearly at the very extremes of a wide spectrum of educational opinion. The Plowden Committee (1967) reported having received some representations from teachers on this topic, which were very similar to the second of the above quotations.

In considering parental interest in their children's education, it is useful to distinguish two aspects. First is the interest which parents may show in the progress of their own children. Secondly, parents may wish to feel involved to some extent in the work and life of the school.

Clearly, these two aspects are related and it is difficult to conceive that many individual parents wish to feel involved in the work and life of the school without being interested in their own children's education. On the other hand there are certainly some parents who are interested in their children's progress but have little or no interest in the school's work as such. They may, for example, feel that it is not the parents' place to help raise money for the school because this should be provided by the local authority. They may have no desire to meet the staff or other parents socially. They may feel that meetings organised by the school are dull, boring or irrelevant for them.

There can be no doubt about the value of a personal interest by parents in their children's progress. This is discussed in some detail in Chapter 4 and research evidence now is fairly strong. Furthermore it confirms a view with which every teacher would concur. On the other hand, some teachers have reservations about those links between school and home which go beyond the exchange of information about the individual child. These reservations spring from a concern that increasing parental involvement in the life of the school may threaten the teacher's professional authority within the school. The Plowden Committee concluded that there were no grounds for such concern.

The information gathered in this study on the nature and extent of contact between schools and parents was necessarily limited because this was not a central focus of interest. However, the schools were asked whether (a) they had a parent–teacher association, (b) meetings on educational matters were held, (c) social functions for parents were organised, and (d) the school received from parents substantial help in money, kind or labour.

Overall some 17 per cent of the children were at schools with parent–teacher associations but there were very considerable regional differences. For example, only 12 per cent of the children in the Northern region were at schools with a parent-teacher association, whereas some 30 per cent of the parents with children in schools in the South-Western region of England had this opportunity. The results indicate that schools with infant classes in the four southernmost regions of England more often have parent–teacher associations than do comparable schools in other regions. The pattern of regional differences for the other indications of parent–school contact was broadly similar, although individual regions sometimes change their relative positions. It is well illustrated in Fig. 39 which shows the percentage of children in schools which have meetings for parents on education matters.

In general, the pattern follows the trend of social class differences between the regions; those regions which have a relatively high proportion of middle class parents, notably those south of a line from the Severn estuary to the Wash, also tend to have more parent–school contacts. Perhaps the single most striking regional difference is that between Welsh schools and those elsewhere in Britain. For example, only a quarter of the Welsh children were at schools where meetings on educational matters were held for parents. As will be seen in Fig. 39 this is markedly lower than the next lowest region, the northern region of England with a proportion of 45 per cent. In fact, for each of the specified forms of parent–school contact, the proportion found in the Welsh schools represented in our sample was lower than for any other

Figure 39. Percentage of children in schools which have meetings for parents on educational matters by region and country

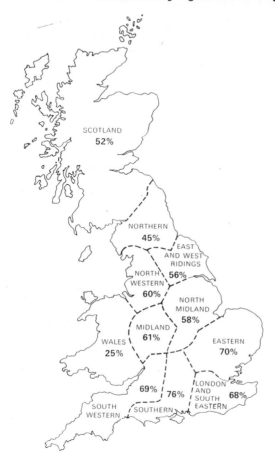

region. Taken together this evidence strongly suggests that parent–school contact at a formal level is less common in Welsh infant and junior with infant schools than elsewhere in Britain. This does not reflect any lack of interest by Welsh parents in their children's education as judged by teachers, as is clear from the results discussed in Chapter 4. Indeed, it is particularly puzzling in the light of the commonly accepted view that Welsh parents as a whole have a very high regard for education. Perhaps this regard is so high that Welsh schools do not feel any need to foster it by arranging any 'formal' meetings for parents. Or perhaps the fact that the schools in Wales were in general smaller than elsewhere means that Welsh teachers are better able to make their contacts with parents in informal out-of-school situations. Or is it that Welsh primary school staff tend to feel that their job is to teach children and not to hold meetings for parents?

The evidence discussed in Chapter 4 showed very clearly the relationship between social class and parental interest. Middle-class parents much more frequently take the initiative to visit the school to discuss their children with the staff. But in the absence of this parental initiative, are the schools successful in persuading parents to come? Apparently not. About 32 per cent of Social Class I parents had come to discuss their children *at the school's instigation* compared with only 24 per cent of Social Class V parents. One might have hoped that efforts by the schools would go some way to redressing the social class imbalance but instead if appears to accentuate it.

Furthermore, this is true of another feature of the results. Middle-class children tend more often to be at schools which have parent–school contacts of the kinds described than do working class children. Thus 89 per cent of the Social Class I children were at schools with at least one of these facilities but only 75 per cent of the Social Class V children. Here are all the hallmarks of a vicious circle: certain sections of the population show a relatively low level of initial interest in education; they do not readily support the attempts which schools make to establish contacts; and the machinery for such contacts tends to wither and with it any hope of awakening interest.

Why are these social class differences so marked? First, and most obviously, middle-class parents tend to place a high value on education. The occupational skills which identify the middle class have often been acquired by extended education and training. Even where this is not the case, the work of the middle-class man usually involves a clerical component, so that the skills which are most highly esteemed in school— reading, writing, number work—are also his occupational tools.

Is this the whole explanation? Probably not. Quite apart from their educational ethos, schools are middle-class institutions. The staff are middle-class by definition and, by and large, this can be seen in their speech, their dress, their values and attitudes. Many parents, whatever their background, have to break through a barrier of some unease in visiting their children's schools. The extremely authoritarian atmosphere of schools in the not-too-distant past may well have left its legacy in the minds of parents. Under such circumstances, any social barrier can serve to intensify the social discomfort. Furthermore, the working class parent may find himself in a minority amongst other parents at formal or social functions. The evidence from a national survey undertaken for the Plowden Committee (1967, Vol. 2) indicated that some working-class parents resent the domination of parent-teacher associations by highly articulate middle-class members.

These results went on to show, first, that parents are more likely to visit the school if the occasion is clearly seen to be relevant to their children or if the children are involved, that is, open days or evenings, school plays, concerts etc. Furthermore, on such occasions working-class parents are much more likely to respond to an invitation than when they are invited to a PTA meeting.

The results discussed in this section are not encouraging. Middle-class parents show a higher level of interest in their children's education than working class parents but there is no evidence that in general any initiatives from infant and primary schools to redress this imbalance have met with success. Middle-class children tend more often to be at schools where there are more or less formalised avenues for parent–school contact. And the distribution of these avenues by region tends to follow the social class distributions.

It is clear that if the situation is to be changed, new initiatives will be needed, new avenues must be explored. In what respects do schools' existing media for establishing contacts with parents fall short? For example, do schools' letters to parents tend to be too impersonal, or often couched in a middle-class idiom?

Experimentation in individual schools and by local education authorities should not prove difficult to evaluate. The yardstick of success is fairly clear: the number of parents who discuss their children's progress with the head- or class-teacher—and, in particular, the number of working-class parents who do so. Evidence from a number of sources suggests that parental attitudes towards their children are at least as important for their children's progress as many of the things which go on inside the school. An educational system which fails to take account of this fact cannot achieve optimum success.

References

CENTRAL ADVISORY COUNCIL FOR EDUCATION (1967) *Children and their Primary Schools* (The Plowden Report) H.M.S.O., 2 vols.
CHALL, J. S. (1967) *Learning to Read: the great debate*, McGraw-Hill.
DOWNING, J. (1964) *The i.t.a. Reading Experiment*, Evans Bros.
FLEMING, C. M. (1959) 'Class size as a variable in the teaching situation', *Educ. Research.* **1**, no. 2.
KEMP, L. C. D. (1955) 'Environmental and other characteristics determining attainments in primary schools', *Brit. J. Educ. Psychol.*, **54**, 145–56.

MORPHETT, M. V. and WASHBURNE (1931) 'When should children begin to read?' *Elem. Sch. J.*, **31**, 496–503.

MORRIS, J. M. (1959) *Reading in the Primary School*, National Foundation for Educational Research.

VERNON, M. D. (1957) *Backwardness in Reading*, Cambridge University Press.

WISEMAN, S. (1964) *Education and Environment*, Manchester University Press.

12. Behaviour and adjustment

Introduction

Consideration of the children's behaviour and adjustment is not confined to this chapter. The Bristol Social-Adjustment Guide score is frequently used elsewhere in the book as a yardstick against which to estimate the effects of a variety of circumstances. Here, this measure of social adjustment in school is examined in more depth in relation to social class and sex differences. In addition, the behaviour of children at home, as reported by mothers, is considered.

Behaviour and adjustment at home

A sceptic might say of mothers' reports of their children's behaviour that they reveal as much about the mothers as the children! No doubt there is an element of truth in this. Certainly, we must not forget the context in which the information was gathered. However, since most reports about children's behaviour at home are given by parents, the information from the study is relevant to the experience of the doctor, the teacher, the psychologist or the social worker.

In order to reduce bias due to prompting by the interviewer, the mothers were not asked whether any aspects of behaviour were causing concern—except as a supplementary question. Instead, they were questioned about specific aspects of behaviour and were asked either whether the behaviour occurred 'frequently', 'sometimes' or 'never', or, where appropriate, whether the behaviour had occurred at all during the last three months.

The questions were preceded by a short explanation of why they were being asked, in order to allay any anxieties that the mothers were being judged and to try to counteract defensive attitudes in the mothers. Nevertheless, it is unlikely that these measures could be wholly effective and there would have been some underreporting of behavioural difficulties.

Sex differences

In general the sex differences 'favour' the girls. Although none of them is very marked when viewed alone, the pattern which emerges is interesting. Boys more frequently showed behaviour which has an aggressive component. This is not unexpected and it is perhaps surprising that the gap between the sexes was not wider. There is some evidence, too, that boys are more restless than girls at this age. Thus, rather more of the boys in the study were reported to have more 'difficulty in settling to anything for more than a few moments'. On the other hand, girls are more likely to suck their thumbs, bite their nails and be 'miserable or tearful'. They are also more likely to be 'faddy' or to have a 'poor appetite'.

What are the reasons for these differences? Although in our society there is a growing tendency for the sexes to move closer together in terms of behaviour, attitude, expectation (even in clothes and hairstyles), the male role is still seen as more dominant than the female. Boys tend to model themselves on the behaviour of men they see around them, particularly their fathers, and girls adopt a feminine role; these tendencies are also reinforced by social pressure from other children.

The physical care of babies and small children is usually in the hands of women. Girls begin to identify with their future role by playing with dolls and these tendencies are anticipated by adults, who give dolls to girls but not boys. The pressure from peers is introduced at a later stage when a boy playing with dolls may be mocked by boys and girls alike, although it is interesting to note the increasing popularity of doll-like soldier figures amongst boys.

In the same way, aggression, rough play and even some disobedience is expected of boys both by adults and by other children. If this aggression is inhibited by society, as it tends to be amongst girls, signs of disturbance are less likely to take overtly aggressive forms. Tearfulness and worrying are passive reactions to conflict situations and are more acceptable in the woman or girl than in the man or boy.

It has also sometimes been suggested that the adoption of the female role for girls is relatively easier than the male role for boys. The tasks which a mother carries out are more evident and easier for children to understand. She is seen to be doing a variety of household jobs, such as cooking, making beds and mending clothes. On the other hand, the father's work is normally out of the child's sight. Father usually disappears after breakfast and reappears for the evening meal. His job—particularly if it is a non-manual occupation—may be difficult for children to comprehend. Even if it is relatively straightforward to explain in general terms, it may be less easy for a boy to replicate in imaginative play. And it is unlikely to suggest the variety of tasks which are undertaken by the mother.

How then is the boy to imitate his father in imaginative play? What is the essence of the male role with which he is expected to identify? How can he practise being a man? Everything that we know about the adjustment of children and of adults indicates that they are happiest when they know what is expected of them, what their points of reference are. If, then, for boys—and particularly for younger boys—these points of reference are less clearly demarcated, good adjustment is perhaps more difficult for them to attain.

The relatively greater frequency of thumb-sucking and nail-biting in girls is interesting because this sex difference is unlikely to be socially determined by imitation of adult behaviour. It is true that once a sex difference is established it could be sustained by peer group pressures. Thus, smaller boys could be inhibited from persisting in these habits because older boys less often have them. However, it is difficult to see how or why these sex differences are established at all. Thumb-sucking is rarely seen amongst adults and finger-sucking is usually well disguised. Both habits in children could be seen as oral gratification but there seem to be no cogent reasons why girls should turn to them more than boys except again that they are passive activities. Perhaps nail biting can be viewed as aggression directed towards oneself in the absence of acceptable alternative outlets.

Social class differences

If this latter explanation were correct, however, one might expect that middle-class children, who show notably less overt aggression than working-class children, would also more often bite their nails. But the social class gradient is in the opposite direction, with 8 per cent reported to be frequent nail biters in Social Class I compared with 13 per cent in Social Class V. It is certain that social pressure in middle class families would be directed to eliminating this 'bad habit'. Does this pressure override more basic tendencies?

If it does, it is less successful in eliminating thumb sucking, for here the social class gradient is in the opposite direction with 10 per cent of Social Class I children reported to be frequent thumb suckers and only 5 per cent amongst manual workers. Is the relative popularity of 'dummies' or 'comforters' amongst working-class groups the explanation of this finding? If so, perhaps those parents who find the sight of a 'dummy' aesthetically displeasing should weigh this against any aesthetic objections to thumb-sucking! The arguments against the use of a dummy on hygienic (as distinct from dental) grounds have always seemed rather slender in view of the multitude of other objects which inevitably find their way into young mouths.

For other aspects of behaviour assessed in the study, where there were social class differences, behavioural 'difficulties' are more frequently found in the working-class groups. In interpreting these results, however, we should avoid the trap of attempting to impose middle-class values on all the children. For example, the results show that aggression in various forms is more frequently seen in the working-class groups at this age. This may well indicate that overt aggression is more acceptable in these groups than among, say, professional workers and their children. Thus the mother of a working-class family may not view a temper tantrum as a serious difficulty. In the school situation, however, temper tantrums or fighting with other children is not only more disruptive but is also more at variance with the standard of behaviour which teachers expect of their pupils. The possible implications of this for teachers are discussed in the next section but the significance of aspects of behaviour in individual children may vary with their social group. For example, the destruction of others' belongings may be an indication of emotional problems in the child of parents of professional status because it is grossly at variance with what is expected of the child at home as well as at school. In a child from an unskilled working-class family, destructiveness may also indicate emotional problems but in view of the fact that such behaviour is five times as common in this social group as in the professional group, it may only indicate that this particular behaviour is more accepted at home.

There is one other feature of the social class differences in children's behaviour at home which is of interest because it contrasts with the picture which emerges at school. The results suggest a gradient from Social Class I to Social Class V for many aspects of behaviour reported in the home. This gradient does not always appear regular from one social class to another but there are no indications that the step from Social Class III (manual) to Social Class III (non-manual) is consistently accompanied by a marked difference in behaviour. Indeed for some aspects of behaviour there is no difference at all between these two groups.

On the other hand, in examining the results for behaviour and adjustment in school, the gap between Social Class III (manual) and Social Class III (non-manual) does appear marked and consistent as will be shown in the next section, where the possible reasons for this are also discussed.

6

Beha~~viour~~ and adjustment in school

The children's behaviour in school was assessed with the Bristol Social-Adjustment Guide, which was completed for each child, usually by the class teacher. The Guide measures the extent to which a child's behaviour in school deviates from normal. The teacher is presented with a large number of descriptions of behaviour and is asked to underline the descriptions which best fit the child. Essentially, then, the teacher is asked to identify behaviour rather than to assess adjustment.

After the completion and return of the Guide, those aspects of behaviour which show some degree of deviance from normal are identified and given codes. By summing the number of coded items for each child, an overall total is obtained. This total is a reflection of the child's emotional and social adjustment in school: the larger the score, the more deviant behaviour has been noted.

A grouping of scores has been proposed by Stott (1963) and also used by Crawford (1966) and Chazan (1968) amongst others. Children with a score from 0 to 9 are termed 'stable', those with a score from 10 to 19 are termed 'unsettled', and those with a score of 20 or more are called 'maladjusted'. For the sake of convenience and comparability, these groupings and terms are used here, although it is recognised

Figure 40. Percentage of 'maladjusted' children by social class and sex

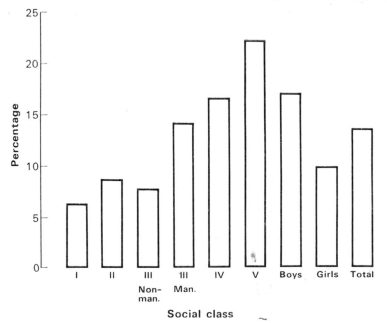

that the terminology is not necessarily applicable in, say, a clinical context.

The percentages of children found to be 'stable', 'unsettled' and 'maladjusted' were, respectively, 64, 22 and 14. Figure 40 shows the sex and social class comparisons of 'maladjusted' children.

We may now return to the discussion commenced in the previous section on the differences between the behaviour and adjustment of middle class and working class children. From the results shown in Fig. 40 it is clear that the prevalence of 'maladjustment' shows a trend from Social Class I to Social Class V. However, this increase is not regular. For example, the difference between the results from Social Class II and Social Class III (non-manual) is so small as to be of little interest. In fact, all the differences between the three non-manual groups are modest in size. But the step from these groups to Social Class III (manual) is a large one. The picture which emerges, then, is of a relatively homogenous non-manual or middle-class group which has a much lower incidence of 'maladjustment' than all of the manual or working-class groups. Of these latter groups, Social Classes III and IV are relatively close together while Social Class V has a much higher prevalence of 'maladjustment' than all the other groups. This situation is not unlike that which was seen for abilities and attainments (see Chapter 10).

However, the pattern of results discussed earlier for the various aspects of behaviour reported by mothers did not indicate that the prevalence of behavioural difficulty changes markedly from working-class groups to middle-class groups.

What are the reasons for these contrasting findings? First, the nature of the measures used is likely to produce such results. The Guide pinpoints deviations from normal school behaviour. 'Normal' in this context will in general be the kind of behaviour that is expected in what is basically a middle-class institution. Of course, many of the behavioural deviations noted in the Guide are abnormal by any standard but a proportion will reflect school norms. Furthermore, the Guide is largely measuring social behaviour and is therefore more likely to highlight social differences. On the other hand, much of the behaviour reported by mothers (e.g. worrying, thumb-sucking, sleeping and eating difficulties, headaches) does not necessarily involve social interaction.

Secondly, there is an obvious difference between the two groups of 'reporters'. Teachers are a relatively homogenous group in this context. In so far as their reports contained a subjective element, this would tend to be uniformly middle-class in outlook, serving again to accentuate middle-class/working-class differences. On the other hand, the group of mothers was as socially heterogenous as the group of children. Furthermore, each individual mother would, of course, share the same social environment as her child. In so far as the mothers' reports contained a subjective element, this would reduce social class differences because they would tend to use the norms of behaviour in their own social group as a frame of reference. Thus, a mother's judgment as to whether her child fought with other children 'frequently' or 'sometimes' would be influenced to some extent by the behaviour of other children known to her. A given number of fights in a week might be described by a middle-class mother as 'frequently' fighting, whilst a working-class mother might describe it as 'sometimes' fighting.

Syndrome scores

Thus far we have been concerned only with a single, overall measure of behaviour and adjustment in school. This, as we have seen, reflects sex and social class differences. But as a measure it is relatively crude because it does not distinguish between different kinds of deviant behaviour. One child with a given score may be aggressive, restless and unco-operative, whilst another with the same score may be withdrawn, timid and anxious.

Figure 41a. Bristol Social-Adjustment Guide 'syndrome' scores by social class and sex

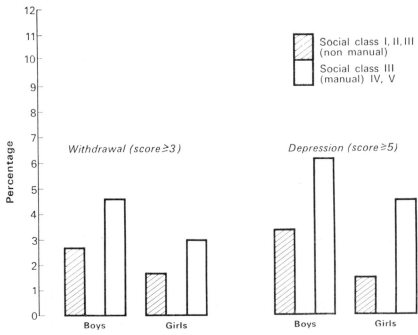

Figure 41b. Bristol Social-Adjustment Guide 'syndrome' scores by social class and sex

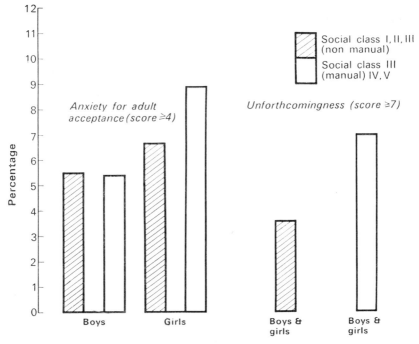

The scoring of the Guide makes it possible to distinguish these and other kinds of behaviour with sub-scores or 'syndrome' scores. Behavioural items showing common tendencies are grouped together to produce 'syndromes' such as 'withdrawal', 'depression', 'hostility towards adults'. Every child has a score on each syndrome which will range from 0 to whatever is the total possible score for that syndrome.

Comparisons were made between boys and girls and between the social classes. The pattern of social class results for the syndrome scores was similar to that seen for the overall score, so the non-manual social classes have been grouped together (middle-class) and the manual social classes also grouped (working-class).

As with the overall score, it was decided to look at children with extreme scores rather than investigate average tendencies. The proportion of children falling into these extreme groups is necessarily a rather arbitrary figure and it was decided to choose scores which cut off as near as possible 6 per cent of the children.

In Figs 41a to e the results are shown for the sex and social class comparisons. They can be summarised as follows:

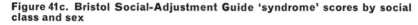

Figure 41c. Bristol Social-Adjustment Guide 'syndrome' scores by social class and sex

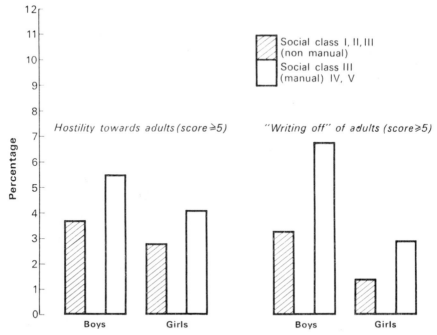

1. The overall pattern is of more boys than girls *and* more working-class than middle-class children showing extremes of behaviour except in (*a*), (*b*) and (*c*) below.

(*a*) Nearly three times more boys than girls showed 'anxiety for acceptance by other children' but there was no social class difference.

(*b*) Twice as many working-class as middle-class children were 'unforthcoming' in their behaviour in school but there was no sex difference.

(*c*) More girls than boys were 'anxious for adult acceptance' and more working-class girls than middle-class girls, but there was no difference between middle-class and working-class boys.

2. The largest social class differences common to both sexes were for behaviour which indicated a 'writing off' of adults or adult standards. For boys and girls there were twice as many working-class as middle-class children.

3. The largest individual difference between groups was for 'inconsequential' behaviour. (Children showing this kind of behaviour appear to have little or no regard for the consequences of their behaviour; they show frequent and recurrent misbehaviour.) Girls overall were much less likely to show this kind of behaviour than boys but the group of

Figure 41d. Bristol Social-Adjustment Guide 'syndrome' scores by social class and sex

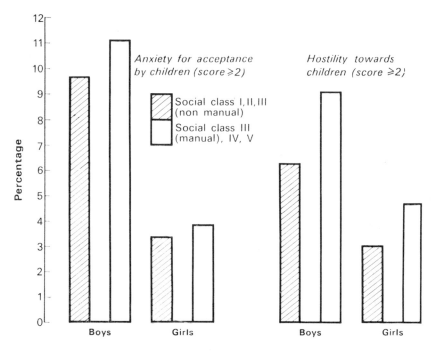

middle-class girls here was strikingly small. Thus, for every one middle-class girl in the category there were four working-class girls, six middle-class boys and ten working-class boys.

The detailed results from the syndrome scores show that the overall pattern of sex and social class differences which emerged from a consideration of the global score on the Guide tends to be sustained when different dimensions of behaviour in school are examined. Of course, the children were only seven years old at the time, but the conclusion seems warranted that boys in general and working-class boys in particular are at higher risk at the primary school stage in terms of their emotional and social adjustment.

Are there any implications in these results for the training of teachers, psychologists, psychiatrists, paediatricians and social workers who are professionally concerned with children? The training of many of these workers gives scant attention to normal child development or to the effect of different child rearing practices in different social groups. But our results confirm that these areas of knowledge are potentially of considerable importance to the professional worker in a number of

Figure 41e. Bristol Social-Adjustment Guide 'syndrome' scores by social class and sex

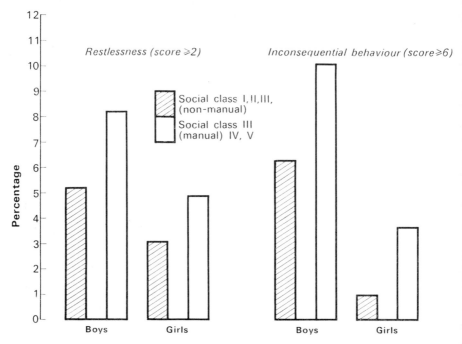

ways. First, the ability to detect the abnormal depends upon knowing what is normal or, to be more accurate, knowing *how normal* particular aspects of behaviour are. Secondly certain kinds of behaviour are relatively common amongst boys and in particular social groups but rare amongst girls and in other groups. Hence the normality or abnormality of behaviour has to be seen within its social setting and taking into account sex differences.

For teachers, who work most closely with children, the social class differences in behaviour pose important educational problems. If some of the behavioural difficulties are in part caused by mal-adaptation to the norms of a middle-class institution (the school), then a detailed knowledge by the teacher of child-rearing practices and their effects in different groups is vital. Further, it might be argued that certain established patterns of behaviour in social groups are well adapted to the environmental circumstances of those groups. Any success the teacher has in modifying behaviour might be accompanied by corresponding difficulties for the child in coping with the demands of his environment outside the school. Perhaps the efforts of the teacher—as well as the psychologist and psychiatrist—should be directed towards helping the child to adapt to the particular environment in which he finds himself. This would involve an acceptance by the adult and ultimately by the child that standards or norms of behaviour are within limits relative and that particular codes of behaviour are in no absolute sense the 'right' ones.

National and regional differences

It has been shown that sex and social class differences in behaviour and adjustment are often very marked. What of regional and national differences?

The overall relevance of regional comparisons was discussed in Chapter 1 but they are of particular importance and interest in relation to behaviour because of the light they may shed upon child rearing practices and upon community attitudes. They may also reflect temperamental differences between children in different parts of Britain. Although the origins of the behaviour must remain speculative as far as the present study is concerned, research specifically directed to these questions could go further.

One of the principal difficulties in interpreting regional and national differences is that Wales and Scotland and the regions of England vary very considerably in their social class composition (see p. 8) and in many other respects. Comparisons between children in different parts of Britain should be designed to make allowance for these social and other factors otherwise differences noted might be more apparent than real.

Time has so far permitted this detailed analysis only for a comparison of the behaviour of English, Welsh and Scottish children in respect of their social adjustment in school (e.g. p. 33). This showed that when allowance was made for other relevant factors, Scottish children are better adjusted in school than Welsh children, who in turn are better adjusted than English children (at seven years of age).

National differences have been analysed in respect of a few aspects of behaviour at home, when allowance was also made for social class differences. For example, English and Welsh children were found more often to be reluctant to go to school than Scottish children. Similarly, Scottish children were reported less often to have temper tantrums than their counterparts in England. Finally, English children were more often said to 'worry about many things' than Scottish or Welsh children.

In addition there are a number of national and regional differences which cannot be explained in terms of social class differences because the trends are in opposite directions.

The popular stereotype of a Scot (except in Scotland!) is that he is rather dour, phlegmatic and unemotional, while the Welshman tends to be thought of as being rather emotional and quick to respond. The Englishman is seen by the outsider as perhaps nearer to the Scotsman than the Welshman and is thought to be rather restrained, keeping his feelings well under control. Is there any basis for these stereotypes in the children's reported behaviour? Some 13 per cent of the Welsh children were said to be frequently 'irritable, quick to fly off the handle' compared with 11 per cent of English children and only 8 per cent of the Scottish children. The difference between the Welsh and English children is relatively small but it is in the opposite direction from that which would be expected from the social class difference, as is the larger gap between the Scottish children and the other two groups. Similarly, 44 per cent of the Welsh children were reported by their mothers to be 'sensitive or highly strung' compared with 39 per cent of the English and 35 per cent of the Scottish children. Social class differences here are minimal.

This latter question proved to be rather undiscriminating, probably because it was not specific and was too open to subjective interpretation. However, it is interesting to speculate how far the answers to the question were a reflection of what the Scottish, Welsh and English children were actually like and how far they reflect the value which their mothers place upon 'sensitivity'.

In relation to attitudes to school there are fairly clear differences which run counter to social class trends. Thus, 76 per cent of the Scottish children were reported by their teachers to have settled down within a month of starting school. On the other hand, the corresponding percentages in the four southern-most regions of England were around 68 per cent. When mothers were asked the same question, higher percentages were obtained but the differences were in the same direction. Approximately 7 per cent of the children in England were said by their mothers to be 'unhappy at school' or 'not altogether happy' and only 4 per cent in Scotland.

In fact, in general terms the Scottish children appear to be showing less signs of stress or deviant behaviour at this age in school and at home than do children in England and Wales. Many of the differences are relatively small but they are consistent.

Differences in behaviour and adjustment between Welsh children and English children at seven years of age are less consistent.

The analysis of social adjustment in school, however, provided firm evidence that Welsh children at least in this sphere compare favourably with English children and further investigation is indicated.

What is the interpretation of these findings? Is it to be found in the attitudes of Scottish parents towards child-rearing and towards education? The evidence from the study on these points can only be regarded as tentative. However, there are a few pointers. For example, Scottish parents more often read to their seven-year-old children than do parents in England, contrary to what might be predicted from social class differences. Furthermore, when allowance was made for social class, it was found that stated parental aspirations for their children's education were higher amongst Scottish and Welsh parents than amongst the English.

One of the aims of large-scale studies should be to point the way to profitable lines of research on a smaller scale and in more depth. The further study of regional and national differences in children's behaviour and in parental attitudes and expectations is surely one such field.

Records of child-rearing practices in different primitive cultures by social anthropologists have in the past thrown a great deal of light upon the relationship between early experience and later developments. The practical difficulties and cost of undertaking cross-cultural studies in Britain are much less and could yield worthwhile material.

References

CHAZAN, M. (1968) 'Symposium: Recent Research on Maladjustment', *B.J. Ed. Psych.*, **38**, Part I, 5–7.

CRAWFORD, A. (1966) Department of Psychology, Liverpool University. Unpublished communication.

STOTT, D. H. (1963) *The Social Adjustment of Children: Manual to the Bristol Social-Adjustment Guides*, University of London Press.

13. The children who died or suffer from serious defects

Overall mortality

Of the original cohort of 17,418 births which formed the basis of the present study, 389 (2·2 per cent) died shortly before or during birth and 280 (1·6 per cent) died during the first four weeks. Fig. 42 shows clearly how mortality is at a peak around the time of birth and then falls

Figure 42. Total mortality rates and deaths due to congenital defects

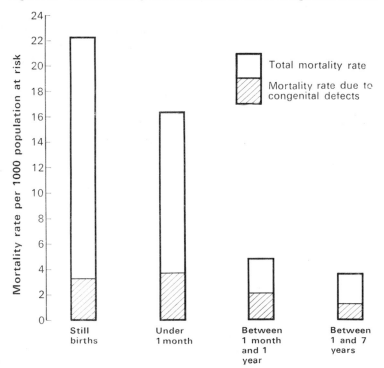

steeply after the first four weeks of life. It also shows the part played by the least preventable deaths—those due to congenital defect. In the very early days of life congenital defects caused under a fifth of the deaths in this study; the majority of deaths were due to immaturity or birth injury. But over the age of a month congenital defects were the cause of over one third of the deaths.

Table 5 gives the numbers and causes of deaths amongst the children in the study aged four weeks to seven years. It must be remembered that these deaths took place between 1958 and 1965, so that they are not necessarily representative of the present state. Furthermore, the total number of deaths is too small for detailed analysis. As has been said, congenital defects were the cause, or associated cause, of more than a third of these deaths. Infections caused the same proportion of deaths but two other important causes were accidents and malignant disease (cancers and leukaemia).

Congenital and other serious defects: incidence, survival and disability

The importance of congenital and other defects lay not only in the deaths they caused, but also in the disabilities they caused in the survivors. Furthermore, in assessing the future prevalence of congenital disability, one must recognise that with present standards of medical care the survival of disabled children will be considerably prolonged and furthermore that many who were stillborn in 1958 would have

Table 5. Number and causes of deaths occurring between four weeks and seven years

Cause of death	Number of children		
	Boys	Girls	All
Congenital defect	21	29	50
Cerebral palsy/birth injury	4	3	7
Intussusception	2	0	2
Malignancy	5	5*	10*
Infection	31	21	52
Asphyxia/inhaled vomit	3	2	5
Accident	8	7	15
Cause unknown	—	3	3
All	74	69	143

* One mongol is included here and in the category of congenital defect but only counted once in the total.

Table 6. Numbers and incidence of serious defects which were congenital or arose at or shortly after birth (excluding defects of the special senses)

Congenital disorder	Stillbirths and deaths before 4 wks	Deaths 4 wks to 7 yrs	Number in NCDS	Alive at 7 years		All†	
				Corrected number†	Incidence per 1000	Corrected number†	Incidence per 1000
Anencephalus	32	—	—	—	—	32	1·8
Spina Bifida and/or Hydrocephalus	42	14	15	18‡	1·1	74	4·2
Heart or blood vessels	36	19	56	60	3·6	115	6·6
Cleft palate	1	—	23	25	1·5	26	1·5
Club feet	21	—	48	51	3·1	72	4·1
Dislocated hips	1	—	17	18	1·1	19	1·1
Other bones or joints	9	1	24	26	1·6	36	2·1
Other malformations	115	3	34	37	2·2	155	8·9
Mongolism	14	7	11	14‡	0·8	35	2·0
Other 'severe subnormality'	—	—	23	25	1·5	25	1·4
Cerebral palsy	—	5	36	39	2·3	44	2·5
Cancer, leukaemia or other tumour	—	10	4	4	0·2	14	0·8
Other congenital disorders	1	9	29	31	1·9	41	2·3
Total children (some have more than one defect)	144	67	398	426	25·6	637	36·6
No. in cohort	669	143	15496*	16606		17418	

* Includes 643 children not matched with perinatal cohort.
† Each total incidence has been corrected to allow for defects estimated to be present in untraced children.
‡ For Spina Bifida and mongolism the actual number amongst the untraced children is known, because they were diagnosed at birth.

survived in 1971. It is therefore imperative, when estimating future prevalence, to take into account the children who some years ago died from congenital defects, hereditary or malignant disease. Since this study represents one week's births, fifty-two times as many defects could be expected in one year in England, Wales and Scotland.

Since defects of vision, hearing and speech have been discussed elsewhere they are not included in this section.

Overall incidence of serious and congenital defects

The total incidence of these defects is given in Table 6, which includes an estimate of the loss due to the untraced children in the cohort. The categories in this table are not mutually exclusive, so that for instance a child with mongolism may occur both under that category and under that of congenital heart disease. It can be seen that 3 to 4 per cent of the *total births* in this cohort suffered from, or developed, serious defects (other than of the special senses). Two-fifths of all the children with these defects died before the age of seven, so that in the surviving children there remained about 2·6 per cent with defects of a serious or potentially serious nature, which were detectable by this age.

Malformations of the brain and spinal cord

More than 1 in 200 (0·6 per cent) of the total births fell into this category. About a third of these had anencephaly, a malformation of the brain which is lethal before or within hours of birth. The remaining children in this group suffered from a malformation of the spine and spinal cord (spina bifida) often associated with 'water on the brain' (hydrocephalus). These conditions are often lethal, or lead to severe mental and physical handicap. In this survey less than a quarter of the children with spina bifida survived to the age of seven, sixteen in all, and of these most had undergone serious operations. Of the sixteen survivors at birth three have not yet been traced, five were in special schools for the physically handicapped, one was recommended for remedial teaching and seven were well and leading a normal life.

In addition to these, two other children had hydrocephalus, one as part of a hereditary condition; the cause of the second child's defect was not known. Both were thought to have an IQ of below 50; one child was attending a training centre, the other lived permanently in hospital.

We may sum up by saying that of the children with known malformations of the brain and spinal cord, only 17 per cent (18 out of 106) survived to seven years, and only 7 per cent (7 out of 106) were leading a normal life.

Malformations of the heart or great blood vessels

Nearly 0·7 per cent of the total births had malformations of the heart or great vessels. In most cases the diagnosis was made at post mortem examination, or after the age of one year. In only a minority was the condition suspected at birth. Only half of the affected children survived to seven years, and fifty-six were traced and included in the study.

About half the survivors had no symptoms at the age of seven, although they were at risk of developing symptoms later in life; about one-quarter were affected or severely handicapped by their heart condition. Six children had multiple handicaps, including deafness, cataract and bony malformations, and an additional four were mongol children. Excluding the mongols, at least seven of the surviving children with heart disease were formally ascertained as in need of special educational treatment.

Malformations of the bones or joints

Some 0·7 per cent of the total births had serious malformations of the bones or joints. About two-thirds of these children survived to the age of seven years.

Seventeen of the seven-year old children, approximately 0·1 per cent, had a history of dislocated hips. Most of these had been treated successfully by long periods of immobilisation in plaster, although at least one still had a limp. Five of the affected children had other defects; one suffered from a generalised disease of the bones; three were mentally retarded and of these one also had a cleft palate, and another had bony defects; and yet another had dorsal kyphosis (hunchback).

Many of the births were suspected of having malformations of the feet, but most were very mild and easily correctable. However, forty-eight of the seven-year-olds had had some degree of clubfoot, about 0·3 per cent, and of these most had been treated by operation, immobilisation in plaster, or calipers. Eight of these children still had a limp at seven years, but most were reported to be walking normally. In three others, additional defects were present: fits, cerebral palsy and mental defect, respectively.

A variety of other bony defects were reported, four children had a shortening of the limbs (although this was before the days of thalidomide); and there were several minor but handicapping abnormalities of the fingers.

Cerebral palsy

Approximately 1 in 400 (0·25 per cent) of the total births were diagnosed as having had or were known to be suffering from cerebral palsy. This is a collective name which comprises a variety of different conditions. All have in common a nonprogressive interference with the normal functions of the nervous system which arises before or during birth or in early infancy. Many but not all these children are mentally retarded, but there are cases where only one or two of the limbs are affected and the child is otherwise quite normal. The majority of the *diagnosed* affected children survived. It is however probable that many of the infants that died during or shortly after birth might well have had a form of cerebral palsy had they survived.

Thirty-six seven-year-old children in the study had a form of cerebral palsy. Only one of these cases was known to have followed an infection (tuberculous meningitis) in infancy. It is notoriously difficult to assess the intelligence of the most affected children because of their speech and motor disabilities, and sometimes visual or hearing defects. Nevertheless, the reported performance of this group makes depressing reading. Four children were stated to have an IQ of 50 or less, and an additional five children were not receiving any education although no comment was made about their mental status. A further eight children were stated to be mentally retarded. Thus nearly half the affected children were reported to be mentally retarded, or apparently so severely handicapped as to make education impossible. Many of the remaining children had difficulties with speech or with co-ordination, although some were said to be improving.

Cleft palate or hare lip

The incidence of cleft palate or hare lip amongst total births was approaching 0·2 per cent. Only one died and information is available on twenty-three of the children surviving at the age of seven. In all but two we know that the defect was surgically repaired, and in the remaining two this question was not answered. In at least three children this defect was only one of multiple malformations, and another child is now known to be in a hospital for the mentally subnormal; yet another also had an abnormality of the hips and was in a hip plaster for some time. In a further four children chronic nasal and ear infections were complications, together with hearing difficulties.

These children therefore had many difficulties to cope with apart from cosmetic and speech problems.

Mongolism

Nearly 0·2 per cent of the children were reported to be mongols (Down's syndrome). Almost a half of these died before the diagnosis could be confirmed, leaving only eleven children known to be mongols at the age of seven, and a further three suspected cases who were not traced.

All but one of the seven-year-old mongols were receiving special education at training or occupation centres. One, who also had deformities of the hands and feet, was attending an ordinary school. At least three of the children also had congenital heart disease, and another had malformations of the legs.

Other congenital defects

Numerous other congenital defects were found in the study; 0·3 per cent of the children had serious defects of the urinary or genital system, but less than a quarter of these survived, of whom ten were traced and included in the study. Of the survivors the majority had chronic urinary infections, and several had had major operations.

Malformations of the gastro-intestinal system were slightly less common, and more than a quarter of affected children survived, eleven children being included in the study. Again several of these had had major operations.

Other types of malformation or defect were less common; there were two children with deficiencies of pigmentation: one a true albino with only partial sight. Two children had a malformation or absence of an ear with hearing loss. Three were born thyroid deficient (cretinism), all of whom were mentally retarded in spite of treatment. Three survivors had fibrocystic disease, but at least seven children with this condition had died before seven years. Two children with muscular dystrophy, eight with cataracts, three with diabetes, and numerous other single instances of rare congenital disorders including haemophilia and a sex disorder were included in the study at seven years.

Acquired defects

The defects which have been so far described have been those present before, during or shortly after birth. However, a number of children developed other serious conditions after birth.

Amongst these were children who had suffered serious accidents. We have already shown that fifteen children, about 0·1 per cent, died accidentally before their seventh year. About half of these deaths occurred in early infancy, and usually no obvious cause was found— although in at least one case the child was reported to have suffocated on a pillow and another had been strangled by his cardigan which had caught on the cot-side. One child died of burns, another was drowned, and the remainder died after road accidents. Several children survived accidents, but were permanently handicapped. Four children had lost an eye before the age of seven, and another had his eye removed because of a detached retina. Eight children were severely scarred after burns or scalds and two had fits after fractures of the skull; two more had slightly paralysed hands after cuts with broken glass.

One of the most common of severely handicapping conditions in the seven-year-olds was a hip disease (Perthé's disease), which sometimes entails treatment for a year or more by immobilisation in plaster or lying on a frame. This was reported in no less than fourteen children, most of whom were in hospital at the age of seven. At least three other children had a persistent limp after an infection of the hip-joint or bones of the leg.

Other serious and progressive illnesses found in the survivors were chronic diseases of the kidneys in three children, and in four more, a form of cancer. Ten children had already died before the age of seven from leukaemia or malignant tumour.

Defects which were educationally handicapping

It has already been made clear that not all of the children with defects were handicapped by them at the age of seven. In some cases the defect had been cured, in others the full effects were yet to be felt. Others, such as the diabetics, were managing well but needed constant medical treatment. Furthermore, there were of course children who without obvious cause were mentally retarded, or were so maladjusted as to need special educational treatment.

In order to identify the children whose defects were proving a handicap to normal education, the teachers and doctors were asked first whether the child was attending or recommended for a special school or unit or receiving special help. Secondly, they were asked whether, if the child was not in one of these categories, they considered he would benefit at that time from special educational help.

A total of thirty-four seven-year-old children were severely subnormal and were either receiving no education at all, were in subnormality hospitals or attending training centres. Another 186 children had either been formally ascertained as in need of special educational treatment, or were attending special schools or units. Together these 220 children amount to over 1 per cent of the whole sample. In addition as many again fell into the category the teachers considered would benefit from special schooling.

Of the thirty-four severely subnormal children at home, in subnormality hospitals, or in training centres, only five had no obvious associated physical manifestation of disease or malformation.

Nearly two-thirds of the 186 children referred to above had some physical manifestation of disease or defect. In the remainder mental retardation was apparently the sole defect, and in the majority of these adverse social or environmental factors seemed to be associated with the backwardness.

The latter comment also applied to those children in ordinary schools whose teachers thought would benefit from special schooling. Among these only a small proportion, about a fifth, were reported to have any physical abnormality; and mental backwardness accounted for the vast majority. On looking at the educational material for these children it became clear that the teachers had included both those with the lowest possible rating on all measures of achievement, and others who had higher ratings but who were not apparently achieving their true potential. This then is a somewhat mixed group, and again very much affected by social and environmental factors.

Comparisons with other studies

With a sample of this size it is possible to compare the prevalence of various conditions with figures obtained from other studies. It is of course important to remember that there is no exactly comparable sample aged seven years, and that most government publications, for example, refer to children aged between five and fifteen. Furthermore, close comparison is never possible unless the same questions are asked in the same way. Nevertheless, bearing these strictures in mind, it is a useful exercise to compare available data, first for a validation of our findings, and secondly, to see whether any notable trends over the years can be detected.

For instance it is important to determine whether the prevalence of severely handicapping conditions is changing. One could argue that with improved obstetric care and a reduction in the number of birth-damaged children the prevalence should be falling. Alternatively it has been said that, since we are now keeping alive children who some years ago would have died, the prevalence should be going up. Only repeated studies of prevalence over the years can give us the answer to this question, which is of vital importance for the planning of provision for the affected children.

In theory, one of the easiest of the handicapped groups to detect should be the 'severely subnormal' children. This term is usually applied to children known, or suspected to have an IQ of below 50. Kushlick (1966) has found that virtually all these children will require special services throughout their lives, and most will eventually need residential care. The prevalence of this condition in children in England has recently been investigated in three different areas, (Kushlick, 1965; Susser and Kushlick, 1961; Goodman and Tizard, 1962). In the older children, the fifteen to nineteen range, all three studies have found a prevalence of about 3·5 per thousand. The authors have argued that this is probably the true prevalence. The fact that the prevalence found in younger children is lower, 0·53 per thousand at ages from birth to four (Kushlick and Cox, 1967), 2·6 per thousand at ages five to nine (Goodman and Tizard, 1962) has been interpreted to mean that a proportion of the younger affected children have not yet been brought to the notice of the authorities or been fully investigated.

For his Wessex study Kushlick (1965) defined the severely subnormal group as follows: those whose most recent IQ score was below 50; those whose scores were unrecordable at testing; who were graded at that time as idiot or imbecile by medical officers; and mongols without IQ scores. In the present study, using the same criteria, it is found that the prevalence of severe subnormality amongst the seven-year-old children traced and included in the study was 2·4 per thousand. On the other hand, it was known that the untraced children included three suspected mongols and two children with a severe degree of spina bifida and brain involvement. If we add these, the prevalence in the total surviving cohort was at least 2·6 per thousand, the same as that reported by Goodman and Tizard for children aged five to nine in 1960. Probably it was somewhat higher than this, for it is likely that there would have been a few severely subnormal children amongst the untraced group without characteristics that would have identified them at birth. We may conclude then that the prevalence of severe subnormality amongst seven-year-olds in 1965 was very similar to what it had been in 1960, and almost certainly no lower. As in all reported recent series mongols made up a third of this group, with a prevalence rate of 0·8 per thousand in surviving seven-year-olds. It will be possible to draw further con- clusions when the data for the eleven-year-olds in the study have been analysed.

The prevalence of all types of cerebral palsy in the present study was 2·4 per thousand, if anything higher than the prevalence reported by Henderson (1961).

The prevalence of congenital heart disease at 7 years was 3·6 per thousand, higher than 2·2 per thousand that was reported in school children in Liverpool (Hay, 1966). This difference may well be accounted for by the remarkably high proportion of children receiving special medical examinations for this study.

In general it can be said that the prevalence of recognisable defects is very similar to that of earlier studies, and that there was, in 1965, no sign of a drop in incidence of severely handicapping conditions. By the age of seven almost two in every hundred children had a serious defect, even before including defects of the special senses or the more common handicap of moderate or mild mental retardation.

References

GOODMAN, N. and TIZARD, J. (1962) 'Prevalence of imbecility and idiocy among children', *Brit. Med. J.*, **1**, 216–19.

HAY, J. D. (1966) 'Population and clinic studies of congenital heart disease in Liverpool', *Brit. Med. J.*, **2**, 661–7.

HENDERSON, J. L. (1961) *Cerebral Palsy in Childhood and Adolescence: a medical, psychological and social study*, Livingstone.

KUSHLICK, A. (1965) 'Community services for the mentally subnormal', *Proc. Roy. Soc.*, **58**, 374–9.

KUSHLICK, A. (1966) 'A community service for the mentally subnormal', *Social Psychiatry*, **1**, 73–82.

KUSHLICK, A. and COX, G. R. (1967) 'The ascertained prevalence of mental subnormality in the Western Region on 1st July, 1963', *Proc. of the Congress of the International Association for the Scientific Study of Mental Deficiency*, 1st, Montpelier, 661–3.

SUSSER, M. W. and KUSHLICK, A. (1961) *A Report on the Mental Health Services of the City of Salford for the Year 1960*, Salford Health Department.

14. The effect of birthweight, gestation and other obstetric factors on disabilities at the age of seven

In these final chapters we examine the relationships between the circumstances surrounding the birth of the children and their subsequent development. The results of the Perinatal Mortality Survey (Butler and Bonham, 1963) confirmed beyond doubt that certain perinatal circumstances, notably variations in birthweight or length of pregnancy, but also adverse social factors and high birth order substantially increased the risk of stillbirth or neonatal death. These general effects must be distinguished from rare disasters which may follow acute complications during pregnancy or labour, and which lead almost inevitably to perinatal death.

In recent years there has been a mounting interest in the effects which these adverse socio-biological factors at birth may have on the subsequent development of the surviving children. This is not only of academic interest. Thus a prolonged pregnancy can be avoided by obstetric intervention, as can a pregnancy threatened by a complication such as high blood pressure. We also know that about a third of the babies of low birthweight are light not because they are born too early but because their intrauterine growth rate has been slowed down. Important amongst causes of this 'slowing down' is smoking during pregnancy, potentially an easily avoidable aspect of maternal behaviour. It is therefore of considerable importance to investigate the long-term consequences of such factors. Moreover, the rapidly increasing survival rate of children who are born long before they are due makes the study of *their* subsequent development important.

The effect of duration of pregnancy

Figure 43a shows the pattern of perinatal mortality in 1958 in relation to the pregnancy. The least risk was when duration of pregnancy was between thirty-seven and forty-two weeks. At either extreme however, when pregnancy had ended more than three weeks before or after the

Figure 43. Duration of pregnancy in relation to (a) perinatal mortality (b) 'educational backwardness'* and (c) 'clumsiness'**

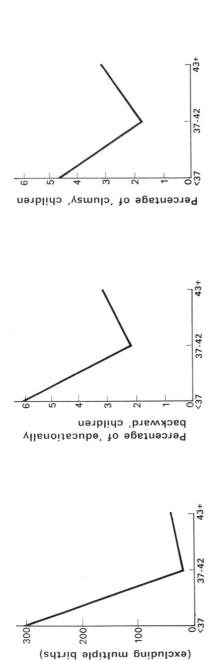

Gestation in completed weeks of pregnancy

*'Educationally backward' children are those who are severely subnormal; in special schools for the educationally subnormal; who have been ascertained as in need of such schooling; and those judged by teachers to need special schooling.

**'Clumsy' children are those judged to be 'certainly clumsy' by their teachers expected duration of two hundred and eighty days the risk of perinatal death was increased.

A very short pregnancy carried an extremely high perinatal mortality risk in 1958: eight times above the average, when the pregnancy ended more than three weeks before the expected time. Moreover, as is shown (Fig. 43b) survivors are at an increased risk of 'educational backwardness'. Even the milder difficulties, such as clumsiness (Fig. 43c) are more common in these children.

For the babies born three or more weeks late, the perinatal mortality rate, though much lower than that for short pregnancies was still nearly twice that of babies born between thirty-seven and forty-two weeks. Further, educational handicap and clumsiness are also commoner in the children born after a prolonged pregnancy.

Duration of pregnancy is related to both birth order and social class; working-class mothers and those having their fifth (or later) child tend to go into labour either too early or too late (Butler and Alberman, 1969). Since educational and physical outcomes are also related to birth

Figure 44. Duration of pregnancy, birth order, social class (1958) and 'educational backwardness'

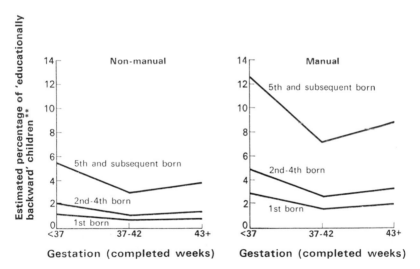

*'Educationally backward' children are those who are severely subnormal; in special schools for the educationally subnormal; who have been ascertained as in need of such schooling; and those judged by teachers to be in need of special schooling.

**Note that these are 'smoothed' percentages obtained from the statistical analysis

Figure 45. Duration of pregnancy, social class (1958), birth order and 'poor copying designs' score (0–4)

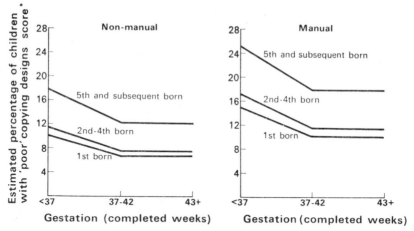

Gestation (completed weeks)   Gestation (completed weeks)

*Note that these are 'smoothed' percentages obtained from the statistical analysis

order and social class these must be allowed for before examining the relationship between either shortened or prolonged pregnancies and adverse condition at seven years.

Figures 44, 45 and 46 show the relationship of length of pregnancy to certain outcomes, allowing for both social class and birth order. The analysis was carried out for three 'pregnancy groups'; those born more than three weeks early; three or more weeks late; and the remainder (between 37 and 42 weeks). There were three birth order groups: first born; second, third and fourth births; and those born fifth or later. Finally two social class groups were chosen on the basis of the fathers' occupations in 1958: manual (working-class) and non-manual (middle-class). For the three outcomes discussed below there is a persisting relationship with length of pregnancy after allowing for social class and birth order.

The prevalence of 'educational backwardness' (2·4 per cent overall) was least in the children born at the 'normal' time and raised at both extremes, particularly in early births (Fig. 44). Thus the effect of being born before thirty-seven weeks as opposed to between thirty-seven and forty two weeks is nearly to double the risk of 'educational backwardness'. Where the length of pregnancy was under 37 weeks, 'educational backwardness' was eleven times more common in the fifth or subsequent children of working-class families (13 per cent) than in first born middle-class children (1·2 per cent).

Figure 46. Duration of pregnancy, social class (1958) and clumsiness*

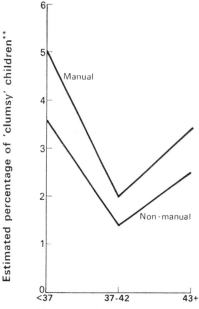

Gestation (completed weeks)

* 'Clumsy' children are those rated as 'certainly clumsy'
by their teachers

** Note that these are 'smoothed' percentages obtained
from the statistical analysis

Early but not late delivery led to a low 'copying design' score
(Fig. 45), after allowing for social class and birth order. Since this test
is also a measure of one aspect of intellectual functioning this finding
tends to confirm the result in Fig. 44.

The prevalence of clumsiness, as rated by teachers, also varied with
length of pregnancy after allowing for social class (Fig. 46). Again, in
terms of the proportions of children affected, the effect of length of
pregnancy was greater amongst the children of manual workers, early
delivery being more deleterious than late, but in this case birth order
had no significant effect.

We may conclude therefore that in this study, as in others (Barker and
Edwards, 1967), both shortened *and* prolonged pregnancies have a
deleterious effect on school achievement, educational performance,
and physical co-ordination. Record, MacKeown and Edwards (1969),
however, suggested that the deleterious effect of prolonged pregnancy
was an artefact, apparently due to mistaken dates on the part of the

mothers. In the present study the length of pregnancy as calculated by
the doctor at the first antenatal attendance was checked by direct
questioning of the mother at delivery and discrepant results were dis-
carded (Butler and Alberman, 1969). It is therefore unlikely that mistaken dates could explain the effect of prolonged pregnancy shown in
this study.

Foetal growth and subsequent development

The weight of a baby at birth is of course very closely related to the
duration of the pregnancy. Towards the end of pregnancy the foetal
growth rate slows down in normal circumstances, and indeed the foetus
may even lose weight if pregnancy is unduly prolonged. It is probably

Figure 47. Birthweight for gestation, birth order and 'recognised handicap'*

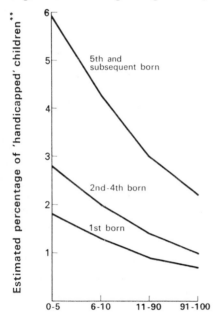

Birthweight percentiles for week
of gestation (> 36 weeks)

*Children excluded from schooling because of
severe subnormality; those already in special
schools for the handicapped; and those
ascertained by Local Authorities as in need of
special schooling

**Note that these are 'smoothed' percentages
obtained from the statistical analysis

Figure 48. Birthweight for gestation, social class (1958), birth order and 'educational backwardness'*

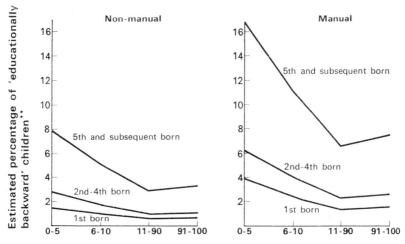

Birthweight percentiles for week of gestation (>36 weeks)

* 'Educationally backward' children are those who are severely subnormal; in special schools for the educationally subnormal; who have been ascertained as in need of such schooling; and those judged by teachers to need special schooling.

** Note that these are 'smoothed' percentages obtained from the statistical analysis

at this time, when the nourishment available has fallen below its optimal level, that a foetus becomes unduly susceptible to birth damage. However, in certain unfavourable circumstances, notably in mothers with raised blood pressure (pre-eclampsia) and in those who smoke heavily, the slowing down of growth rate occurs earlier than usual and often long before delivery is due (Butler and Alberman, 1969). Birthweight considered in relation to the duration of pregnancy (i.e. 'birthweight for gestation') is therefore a sensitive indicator of foetal health and perinatal risk. We have grouped children (boys and girls separately) into four birthweight groups: the lightest 5 per cent, the next lightest 5 per cent, the next 80 per cent and the heaviest 10 per cent, for the completed week of pregnancy. In this way we have standardised for length of pregnancy from the outset. The lightest 5 per cent are often termed 'light for dates' babies.

As with length of pregnancy, there tends to be an optimum group; this is between the 10th and 90th percentiles. It is very much worse for the baby to be at the lighter end, but there is also a suggestion that it is

Figure 49. Birthweight for gestation, social class (1958), birth order and 'poor' copying designs score (0–4)

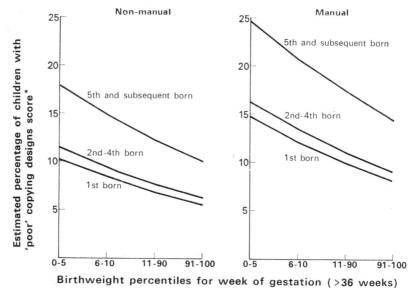

Estimated percentage of children with 'poor' copying designs score*

Birthweight percentiles for week of gestation (>36 weeks)

* Note that these are 'smoothed' percentages obtained from the statistical analysis

sometimes a disadvantage to be 'heavy for dates' (i.e. the heaviest 10 per cent). This pattern holds both for perinatal mortality, and for certain adverse outcomes at the age of seven.

As in the case of short gestation, a low birthweight for gestation is found in association with other adverse birth factors; among these are low social class, and in this case first pregnancies. We have therefore analysed the effect of birthweight for gestation, allowing for the effects of birth order and social class. Since, as we have shown, a birth more than three weeks early carries its own risks, we have excluded all babies born before 37 weeks in order to simplify the interpretation of the following analyses.

Figure 47 shows the results for children with 'recognised handicaps'. In the lightest 5 per cent, the proportion of handicapped children was about twice that in the children lying between the 10th and 90th percentile. The proportion of handicapped children was highest in the fifth and later born children, ranging from 5·9 per cent in the 'light for dates' to 2·2 per cent in the 'heavy for dates' children. Social class was not related to 'recognised handicap'.

However, when the children who were 'educationally backward' were considered (Fig. 48), social class was an important factor. Amongst the most under-privileged children, i.e. fifth or later born children with fathers in manual occupations, the prevalence of 'educational backwardness' amongst the lightest 5 per cent at birth was nearly 17 per cent: two and a half times the prevalence among the children between the 10th and 90th percentile. Among the most privileged children i.e. the firstborn of fathers in non-manual occupations, the prevalence fell from 1·5 per cent in the 'light for dates' group to 0·6 per cent amongst the children between the 10th and 90th percentiles. This is another example of the modifying effect which social factors can have on perinatal circumstances and is similar to the findings relating length of pregnancy to 'educational backwardness'. A very similar pattern is seen in Fig. 49, which illustrates the joint effects of birthweight for gestation, social class and birth order on the score in the copying designs test.

Interestingly, however, clumsiness, which had varied substantially with duration of pregnancy, showed no variation with birthweight for gestation, when allowance had been made for the effects of birth order and social class.

The relationship between other obstetric factors and adverse outcome

Analyses have not yet been carried out in the same detail for other obstetric factors, namely: severe pre-eclampsia; early or late bleeding in pregnancy; foetal distress; prolonged labour; and abnormal method of delivery, for example, vertex occipito posterior, breech, forceps, or caesarean section carried out pre-labour or in labour. Their complex relationship with the maturity of the baby and social class and birth order makes this potentially a very complicated investigation. Nevertheless, a preliminary examination was made for each of these factors in isolation against certain outcomes similar to those discussed earlier in this chapter. These were: 'recognised handicap'; children thought by their teachers to be in need of special schooling; those rated by teachers as certainly or somewhat clumsy; and those with a poor score on the copying designs test. The only important association among all these was between foetal distress and clumsiness. The proportion of handicapped children or those thought to be in need of special schooling was, however, increased amongst those mothers who had not been attended by a trained person in labour.

Heavy smoking in pregnancy is an important factor which has been shown to increase perinatal mortality risk by about 30 per cent (Butler and Alberman, 1969). It has already been shown that there was a persisting effect on the height of the seven-year-old children (Chapter 8).

Preliminary analyses suggested that smoking in pregnancy also increases the risk of those adverse conditions that have been discussed in this chapter. In the following chapter it will be shown that an adverse effect on reading ability and social adjustment persists even when allowance is made for other factors.

In this chapter we have endeavoured to show that the effects of adverse birthweight and gestation are not confined to an increased risk at birth, but extend to the later development of the child. It has been shown that both unduly short and unduly prolonged pregnancies are associated with later handicap, and also with disabilities of a less serious nature. Low birthweight for gestation, too, is associated with later handicap, and other difficulties. Clearly these findings suggest possibilities for preventive action.

An important finding too, is the extent to which social environment may mitigate the effects of adverse perinatal factors. The corollary of this is that socially disadvantaged groups in the community are much more vulnerable to certain adverse perinatal events.

References

BARKER, D. J. P. and EDWARDS, J. H. (1967) 'Obstetric complications and school performance', *Brit. Med. J.*, **3**, 695.

BUTLER, N. R. and BONHAM, D. G. (1963) *Perinatal Mortality*, Livingstone.

BUTLER, N. R. and ALBERMAN, E., eds (1969) *Perinatal Problems*, Livingstone.

RECORD, R. G., McKEOWN, T. and EDWARDS, J. H. (1969) 'Relation of intelligence to birthweight and gestation', *An. Hum. Genet. Lond.*, **33**, 71.

15. Social and biological influences on reading attainment and adjustment in school

In the previous chapter the relationships were investigated between circumstances during pregnancy and around the time of birth and a number of conditions at seven years. However, relatively small extreme groups were being considered (e.g. clumsy children, educationally backward children etc.).

The problem can also be considered in another light; namely, are adverse birth factors associated with lower than average achievement apart from their relationship to the risk of handicap? An analysis on these lines is a more sensitive measure of the effects of birth circumstances on *all* children, and it is possible to take into account many more factors which may influence the final outcome. Therefore it was decided to investigate factors influencing measured reading attainment (Southgate test score) and social adjustment in school (Bristol Social-Adjustment Guide score).

As in previous chapters where complex analyses were undertaken, it was necessary to examine the separate effects of each of the various factors after allowance had been made for a number of other factors which might influence the outcome.

Reading attainment

The combined effects on reading of the following factors were studied: sex, social class, maternal height and age at the child's birth, the mother's smoking habits during pregnancy, length of pregnancy, the child's birthweight, birth order, and the number of younger (i.e. later born) children in the household when the child was seven years old. The results are presented in terms of the gain in months of reading age (Fig. 50). It will be remembered that the size of the estimated effects is to some extent dependent upon the factors included and their categorisation.

It was found that with two exceptions each of the factors included

7

Figure 50. Social and biological factors and reading attainment

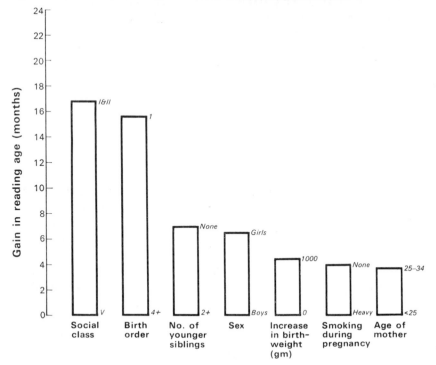

had a separate effect upon reading attainment after allowing for all the others; the exceptions were maternal height and length of pregnancy.

The reader will by now be familiar with the marked relationship between social class and reading attainment. The difference between children from Social Classes I and II and those from Social Class V is equivalent to nearly seventeen months of reading age.

The effect of family size (i.e. number of children in the household under the age of twenty-one) has also been shown previously (p. 32) but the present analysis makes it possible to distinguish between the effects of birth order (or, strictly, the number of previous live and still-births to the mother) and the number of younger (i.e. later born) children. Several workers have commented upon the adverse effects on educational attainment of both high birth order and the number of younger children (e.g. Lees and Stewart, 1957). Our results confirm their findings.

The difference in reading attainment between first born and fourth or later born children is equivalent to sixteen months of reading age and the *additional* effect of having two or more younger siblings is equivalent to a loss of nearly seven months reading age, a difference comparable in size to the average difference between boys and girls.

The latter findings parallel the effects of birth order and the number of younger children on height described in Chapter 8. Presumably, both findings are at least in part a result of the sharing of resources which occurs with increasing numbers of siblings; although the type of 'resource' concerned with reading is perhaps largely that of parents' time and the opportunities for verbal communication with an adult. It is of course also possible that the poorer reading of children from large families is a reflection of the kinds of parents who have large families (see also the discussion on p. 34).

Over and above these effects, it appears that mothers' age is related to children's reading ability; children of mothers between twenty-five and thirty-four years are better readers than those of younger mothers. This may be related to the fact that older mothers tend to manage better in the home and therefore have more time to spare for their children.

Compared with the social class and family size effects, the influence of the birth factors included in this analysis is relatively small, but nevertheless important. Duration of pregnancy and birthweight have been considered both separately and together. Before adding birthweight into this analysis the effect of length of pregnancy on reading was small but clear. After allowing for all other factors except birthweight the best readers were those born at the 'expected' time (between 38 and 42 weeks), and the worst were those born more than two weeks early, the difference being equivalent to about three months of reading age.

The addition of birthweight to the analysis accounted for the effect of gestational age so that the latter no longer had a significant effect on reading. The effect of birthweight in the analysis is to reduce reading age by four months for every 1,000 gm reduction in birthweight.

It was indicated in the previous chapter that cigarette smoking in pregnancy is related to educational backwardness in children. However, the analysis described there made no allowance for other factors. The results of the present analysis permit an estimate of the size of the relationship between smoking during pregnancy and children's reading attainment; the difference between the children of mothers who had regularly smoked ten or more cigarettes a day in pregnancy and those of non-smokers, is equivalent to four months of reading age (after allowance has been made for the effects of the other factors).

Social adjustment in school

The measure of social adjustment in school used was the score on the Bristol Social-Adjustment Guide. The absence of a scale, corresponding with that of an age scale for reading attainment, makes the assessment of the results more difficult.

Nevertheless the results from the analysis (Fig. 51) follow a similar pattern to those described for reading. Social class and sex effects on social adjustment have already been described in another context (Chapter 12), and these, together with birth order, are the most important in the present analysis.

There is an association between the length of pregnancy and social adjustment in children when allowance is made for all the other variables except birthweight. It is children who are born early (before thirty-eight weeks) or late (forty-three weeks and over) who are worse adjusted than those born at the right time, the degree of deficit being about equal

Figure 51. Social and biological factors and social adjustment

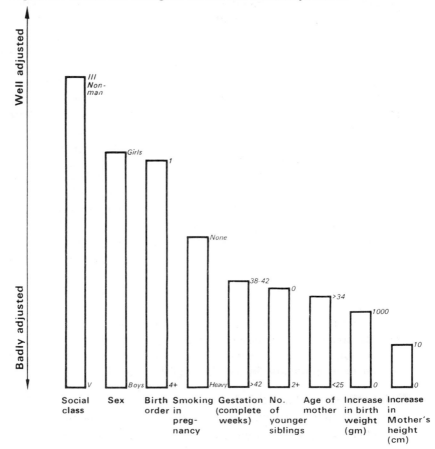

in early and late births and equivalent to about half the sex difference. When birthweight is introduced into the analysis, the gestational effect is still significant but the poorest adjustment is now in those born late (Fig. 51). It is important to note that the effect of lowered birthweight, when allowance is made for gestation, is another aspect of the 'light for dates' effect discussed in Chapter 14.

It is also of interest to note that the number of younger children is associated with adjustment; those children with two or more younger brothers or sisters are less well adjusted in school than those with none. Is the explanation of 'shared resources', advanced in relation to reading attainment and height, still appropriate? It may well be. It can be argued (see also p. 150) that since social adjustment in school is in one sense a measure of conformity to school (i.e. adult) standards of behaviour, those children who have to share their parents' time with more brothers and sisters have less opportunity to learn and adapt to adult standards.

The findings from the two analyses discussed in this chapter provide much room for thought as well as providing answers to many questions. Three results are worthy of particular note in relation to practical implications and the need for further research.

First, children from large families clearly emerge as an under privileged group (see also discussion on p. 34). Secondly, the effect of length of pregnancy on social adjustment is an interesting and potentially important finding. Those children who are born 'early' or who are 'overdue' are less well adjusted than those born 'at term' (for a given social class, birth order, etc.). Also the 'light for dates' have poorer adjustment. Do these findings have implications for obstetricians? For example, prolonged pregnancy is in principle avoidable.

However, any decision to induce labour cannot be taken lightly because of the attendant risks. Not so a mother's decision to stop smoking during pregnancy. It is true, of course, that the findings do not establish a *causal* link between smoking in pregnancy and reading attainment and social adjustment. One cannot rule out the possibility, for example, that the smoking habit may be more common amongst particular groups of mothers whose children are for other reasons progressing less well at school. However, in the present state of our knowledge—and in view of the fact that the perinatal mortality risk is also higher for smoking mothers—it would seem a prudent and urgent task to alert mothers and mothers-to-be to the possible risks involved.

References

LEES, J. P. and STEWART, A. H. (1957) 'Family or sibship position and scholastic ability', *Sociological Review*, **5**, 173–90.

16. The prediction of handicaps and an evaluation of the use of 'at risk' registers

In previous chapters we discussed the prevalence and characteristics of children with defects at seven years; or whose achievements in various spheres, including education, social adjustment and physical dexterity, were considered markedly below normal. We have attempted to relate the abnormalities found at seven to the health and social circumstances of the mother during pregnancy, and to events during birth. This has been done in order to illuminate any causal relationships.

However where the cause cannot be established, or be prevented, the best hope of alleviating the consequences of a defect is by early treatment and therefore early diagnosis. Where defects, or signs of defects, are detectable at birth, diagnosis depends only on the quality of the medical examination. However, defects are often neither visible nor detectable until some time after birth, as for example deafness or mental subnormality. To ensure the earliest possible diagnosis of such 'invisible' defects it is necessary to 'screen' infants and children for signs of such conditions at appropriate stages; in particular it is important to look at those infants who are thought to be at higher than average risk. This is called 'selective screening'.

In order to facilitate this Lindon (1961) and Sheridan (1962) suggested that local authorities keep 'at risk' (or 'observation') registers of children thought to be vulnerable because of adverse circumstances before, during or after birth. Children with a family history of defects, or whose early development gave rise to a suspicion of retardation were also to be added to this register. It was suggested (Sheldon Committee Report, Ministry of Health, 1967) that the 'screening' resources of local authorities should be concentrated on these high risk children, and many areas reorganised their services accordingly.

Latterly, however, some doubt has been cast on the value of such a system (e.g. Oppé, 1967; Richards and Roberts, 1967). The registers have tended to become too large to be of practical use, and substantial numbers of handicaps have been missed in 'low-risk' children who were not on the registers.

One of the main problems lies in the choice and definition of criteria which determine whether or not an infant is considered at high risk of handicap. Furthermore, lack of agreement on definitions, and on standardisation of medical records has made it very difficult to obtain reliable national data either on perinatal or other complications, or on resulting handicaps.

The present study presents a good opportunity for investigating the relationship between birth factors and later handicap. In many respects the study simulates field conditions, perinatal data having been gathered at the time of birth, and follow-up data being based on medical examinations by School Health departments at seven years. Both perinatal and follow-up data are available for over 14,000 children in the study.

In the following account we describe *the measure of success with which it is possible to predict at birth those children in the study who later were shown to be educationally or physically handicapped.* This exercise is closely related to the analyses which have been presented in previous chapters, in the sense that only if there is some link between birth factors and later health or educational status is any prediction possible.

The present account differs from the earlier analyses in one important respect. Children with defects detectable on routine medical examination at birth have, for obvious reasons, been excluded from the 'predictive' exercise, leaving only the 'invisible' defects. This means for example that mongols (Down's syndrome) and children with such defects as clubfeet, cleft palate, and visible defects of the brain or spinal cord, or congenitally dislocated hip, have been excluded, so that the handicapped group has been reduced by nearly one-third.

Our aim has been to select for entry in the register children with that combination of perinatal characteristics which offered the 'best' prediction of later handicap.

The statistical techniques designed to select this 'optimum' at risk group from the data are described elsewhere (Alberman and Goldstein, 1970). There was no information on two factors which are normally available to those operating risk registers, namely family history of defect, and parents' suspicions of retarded development.

The selection of handicaps to be predicted

Two groups of handicap have been selected. The first, *Group A,* has been chosen to simulate as far as possible the type of handicap which most existing local authority risk registers are trying to predict. This group comprised 1·4 per cent of the total sample. It included the children considered to be partially hearing or severely deaf in one or both ears; those ascertained as partially sighted (there were no blind children); those with cerebral palsy, including a few who had died before seven; those excluded from the educational system because of severe mental subnormality; and, finally a small group with multiple defects. These last mentioned children were included even where one defect was of a relatively minor nature since multiple defects often present special educational problems.

Group B, comprised those children who because of educational or mental backwardness were receiving, or thought to be in need of special schooling at the age of seven: 2·3 per cent of the total sample.

The selection of high risk perinatal factors

The object of these analyses, then, was to determine those perinatal factors, which predicted best the children who were subsequently handicapped. The details of these analyses are described by Alberman and Goldstein (1970).

For Group A, after preliminary investigation, five potential predictors were selected for study. Three of these, birth order, the type of delivery and the condition of the baby during the first week, proved to be 'good' predictors (see Table 7); that is to say, they each improved the overall prediction. The addition of the other two factors, namely social class and birthweight-gestation, did not effect any further improvement in prediction.

In effect these findings confirm the commonly expressed view that babies who appear to be perfectly well shortly after birth are, on the whole, unlikely to be suffering from *severe* defects, even of an 'invisible' nature. Furthermore, the findings are in accord with the view that social factors *per se* are not important in this particular group of defects.

Group B comprised the children suffering predominantly from milder forms of mental retardation and excluded the severely subnormal children. Here the position was rather different. The analysis revealed that four factors were important in making the overall prediction: birth order, social class, birthweight-gestation and method of delivery. The fifth factor, namely the condition of the baby during the first week, failed to improve the prediction further. These findings may reflect a situation in which babies of 'adverse' birthweight or gestation were affected, but not sufficiently to produce abnormal signs at birth. Certainly they underline the well-known associations of high birth rank and adverse social factors with educational backwardness.

The optimum size of the 'at risk' group, and the proportion of handicapped children to be expected within the group

Most of the recent work on the practical value of selective screening has concentrated on two crucial questions. What is the optimum size and composition of the high risk group? And, the related question: what proportion of handicapped children will be found in the group? The problem can be simply expressed: if the group is too small it will include only a small proportion of handicapped children, if the group is too large the advantages of selective screening are lost.

Using the present data it has been possible to rank in order various combinations of perinatal factors ranging from those categories where the child is at greatest risk of handicap to those in which the risk is least (see Appendix). Figure 52 gives the relationship between the size of the high risk group and the proportion of handicapped children included for Groups A and B. The high risk groups have of course been so devised

Figure 52. Proportion of handicapped children who would have been on risk registers of different sizes

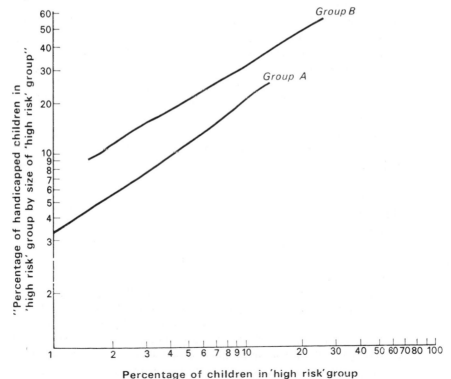

that the smallest contain only those children at greatest risk, and an increase in size is achieved by systematically adding the next most vulnerable categories of children. From this figure it can be seen that it will probably always be difficult to achieve Lindon's (1961) original goal, namely that a high risk group comprising about 20 per cent of all births will include a substantial majority of children later found to be handicapped. The nearest we would come to this would be in the prediction of educational backwardness, where a high risk group of 25 per cent would have included just over half of all the children later found to be affected. The prediction of those children with physical or severe mental handicaps would have been less successful. It must be stressed, however, that we are now considering only perinatal factors, and that clearly if we had added to the high risk group those children whose retarded development in the first year aroused suspicion, prediction would be considerably improved. Nevertheless, even using only perinatal factors it is clear that the high risk groups do include a significantly raised proportion of children later found to be handicapped, and the problem is how to make best use of this information. As explained above, Alberman and Goldstein (1970) discussed this problem and made use of a mathematical model in conjunction with the present data to calculate the optimum size of 'at risk' registers, and the most efficient way in which they could be used. The results of this analysis in respect to the optimum size and composition of the 'at risk' register designed to predict our Groups A, and B, are presented in Table 7.

In these analyses it happens that the *optimum* sizes of the high risk groups are also the *maximum* sizes, given our criteria for entry on the register. Thus for Group A if a baby is of high birth rank *or* has an abnormal delivery *or* shows abnormal signs or serious illness in the first week he should be included on the register in order to achieve optimum prediction. This high risk group comprised 13·2 per cent of all live-births in the sample and a follow-up of these babies would have identified 25·3 per cent of the severe physical, mental or multiple handicaps in the study (Table 7).

Having decided on the size and the composition of the high risk group, the question arises of how to plan the distribution of available resources for screening between the 'high risk' and the remaining children. The mathematical model indicates that the optimum allocation of available resources to detect the maximum number of handicaps depends on the existing rate at which handicaps are being picked up within a given area. For example, Fig. 53 shows that where only a fifth or less of 'Group A handicaps' are at present being detected by a given age it is worth directing *all* resources to the 'high risk' group. However where

Table 7. Optimal groupings for prediction and entry onto 'at risk' register

	Severe physical or mental, or multiple handicap (Group A defined on p. 181)	Educational backwardness requiring special schooling (Group B defined on p. 182)
Prevalence per cent	1·4	2·3
Criteria for entry into the register	1. High birthrank (fifth or later) or: 2. Abnormal delivery (breech, face, internal version or by untrained person) or: 3. Abnormal signs or serious illness in first week (convulsions, cyanotic attacks, cerebral signs, hypothermia, serum bilirubin 15 mgm per 100 cc or more, Rh incompatibility or other serious illness).	1. Illegitimate birth or father unskilled worker or: 2. High birth rank (fifth or later) or: 3. Abnormal delivery (breech, face, internal version or by untrained person) or: 4. Abnormal birthweight or gestation (a) 5½ lb (2,500 g) or less, or born before 37 weeks. (b) Born 43 weeks or later.
Children on register as percentage of all live births	13·2	24·7
Percentage of handicapped children included in register	25·3	53·6

the existing detection rate is greater than a fifth it is always worth dividing available resources between the 'high' and 'low' risk children, always favouring the former but to a decreasing degree as the rate of detection rises. Figs. 53 and 54 show clearly how an optimum division of resources between the high and low risk children will always improve the detection rate *for the same total resources*. Tables in the Appendix give the suggested ratio of resources to high and low risk children for Groups A and B allowing for differences in existing detection rate.

The main conclusions to be drawn from this analysis are that certain carefully selected, yet easily recorded, birth factors are of value in the prediction of handicaps. Furthermore, it can be established that there is always a benefit to be gained from the differential allocation of re-

Figure 53. Differences in detection rates with different distributions of resources: severe physical, mental and multi-handicaps (group A)

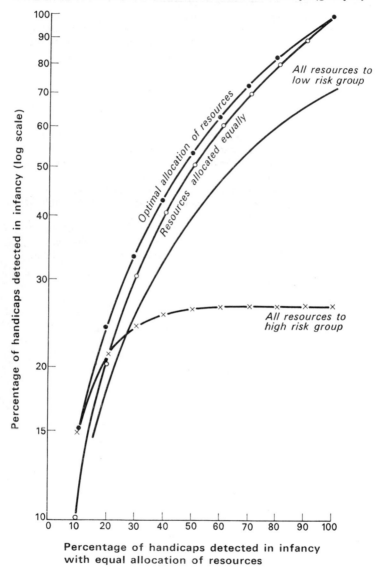

Percentage of handicaps detected in infancy
with equal allocation of resources

sources between children at 'high' and 'low' risk, particularly in authorities where the existing detection rate is low. Clearly, in order to improve the handicap detection rate, it is essential for local authorities to carry out a continuous scrutiny of their data on handicaps and to

Figure 54. Differences in detection rates with different distribution of resources: educational handicaps (group B)

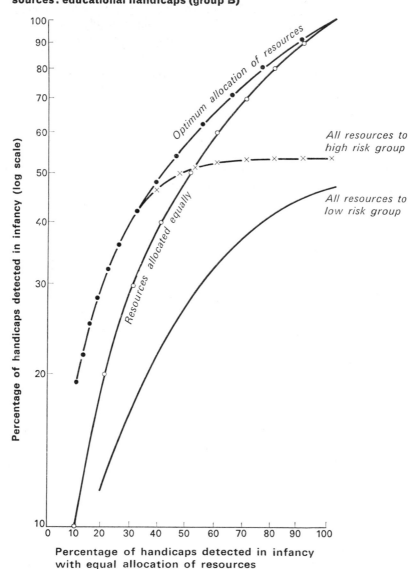

adjust local policy as necessary. No method of prediction can act as a substitute for actual examination of children, but it can at least show the areas where maximum benefit, in terms of detection of handicap, will result when preferential allocation of resources is made.

References

ALBERMAN, E. D. and GOLDSTEIN, H. (1970) 'The "at risk" register: a statistical evaluation' *Brit. J. Prev. Soc. Med.*, **24**, 129–35.

LINDON, R. L. (1961) 'Risk register', *Bulletin, Cerebral Palsy*, **3**, no. 5, 481-7.

HEALTH, MINISTRY OF, (1967) Sheldon Committee Report, H.M.S.O.

OPPÉ, T. E. (1967) 'Risk registers for babies', *Develop. Med. Child. Neurol.*, **9**, 13–21.

RICHARDS, I. D. G. and ROBERTS, C. J. (1967) 'The "at risk" infant', *Lancet*, **2**, 711–13.

SHERIDAN, M. D. (1962) 'Infants at risk of handicapping conditions', *Monthly Bulletin of the Ministry of Health and the Public Health Laboratory Service*, **21**, 238–45.

17. In conclusion

Any attempt to summarise the results comprehensively would be lengthy and perhaps unnecessarily repetitious. At the same time there are a number of features which stand out and which can with advantage be restated in a wider context. In addition, it is appropriate in a final chapter to give some thought to future developments in the study. However, before embarking on a brief consideration of these matters we should answer three questions which may be in the reader's mind.

First, why was the birth week 3 to 9 March chosen as a criterion for selecting this group of children? And, secondly, are the children likely to be different from those born at other times of the year? This particular week was chosen in part because the early spring is the most convenient time in which to mount a national perinatal study; it was unlikely to be affected by very poor weather conditions and few of the many field workers involved would be taking holidays. In addition, the National Survey of Health and Development had started twelve years earlier with a group of children born in the same week.

This latter point is relevant to the second question in that to the extent that there are any differences between children born at different times of the year, comparisons between these two national studies would be unaffected. However, the evidence from this first follow-up indicates that there are no biases in the group which can be attributed to the week chosen. The prevalence of medical conditions, for example, is close to estimates from other sources. In the educational field, it is known that children with birthdays in the autumn term tend to make better progress than those born in the summer. However, the month of March is in the middle of the school year and therefore the children in the study are likely to be average in this respect. Furthermore, the most important findings are concerned with the relationships between various facets of the environment and the children's development. It is difficult to imagine that these would be affected by the time of birth.

There is a third question, which is often raised, namely, does the fact that these children are being studied change them in some ways, so that they are no longer a representative sample? The fact that they have only been studied twice with an interval of seven years between the two occasions makes it unlikely that any such changes could have affected the results so far. However, it is not unlikely that some previously undetected medical, educational or social problems may have come to light as a result of the special attention to the children's development and circumstances at the age of seven. To the extent that this has occurred—and the children have benefited as a result—we would be delighted no matter how 'inconvenient' this might be from a research viewpoint. Of course, this would carry the implication that any estimates of the proportion of children developing adversely in subsequent follow-ups would be minimum estimates.

Nevertheless, there is some evidence from the National Survey of Health and Development (Douglas, 1970) that this 'study effect'—if it occurs—does not influence the overall results. It was not possible for Douglas to follow up all of the children in his birthweek group. However, at the age of eleven and afterwards some of the children who had not been followed up were studied in respect of medical findings and vocational records and no differences were found between these children and the group included in his sample.

Now to turn to more general matters. One of the most striking features which emerges from the results we have presented is the very marked differences between children from different circumstances, which are already apparent by the age of seven. For example, the estimated gap in terms of the average reading performance of the most and the least advantaged children in the analysis in Chapter 15 was over four years. Furthermore, the most potent factors were seen to be located in the home environment. The most obvious implications to be drawn from this are, first, that equality of educational opportunity cannot be achieved solely by improving our educational institutions. Secondly, 'for the culturally under-privileged or deprived child, enriching or compensatory education needs to be provided during the pre-school years and continued during the school years' (Kellmer Pringle, 1969). Wiseman (1970), too, stresses that 'environmental deprivation bears most heavily on the earliest years of childhood; before ever the child reaches the infant school he is already handicapped in the vital area of language development. If nothing is done to remedy this, he arrives at school unable to take advantage of the opportunities offered, the deficit becomes cumulative, and he is permanently lodged in the ranks of the slow learners.'

A second feature of the results, which merits further research, is the wide regional and national variation in aspects of children's development. It is sometimes assumed that such variations can be explained in terms of facilities available or else by the social class differences between regions. However, the results have shown that children in the southern regions of England, favoured in most of the obvious respects, do not always compare favourably with children living farther north. In particular, Scottish children at the age of seven are much more advanced in reading than their English and Welsh counterparts and give every indication of being better adjusted at the age of seven. To what extent can this be attributed to the attitude of Scottish parents to education or to their child rearing practices? How much of the difference can be explained in terms of the expectations and attitudes of Scottish teachers?

The possibility which the study affords for relating the circumstances surrounding the birth of a child to his subsequent development is one of its most important aspects. Our results in this field are encouraging in two respects. First, many obstetric complications, whilst carrying a high risk of perinatal mortality, do not seem in general to be linked to adverse development in surviving children. On the other hand, a number of 'high risk' factors have been isolated and this permits the early identification of a relatively small group of children in whom the risk of handicap is increased. This is not to say that these children should be followed up to the exclusion of others as a relatively large group of handicaps would not have been identified. Indeed, regular observation and screening of *all* children must remain the aim. However, to the extent that this aim is unrealisable in general or in particular areas, some direction of scarce resources to those children at higher risk of handicap seems prudent and we have shown that differential allocation of follow-up resources to 'high' and 'low' risk children is an optimal policy.

A feature of the results, which cannot have escaped notice is that those sections of our community which in general have most need of statutory services tend to use these services least. In Chapter 6 it was shown that children from unskilled working-class families are, for example, least often brought to 'toddler' clinics, to child guidance clinics or to dental clinics. At seven, they are relatively poorly adjusted at school, their dental health is poor and they show signs of delayed development in, for example, bladder control, speech and physical co-ordination. Furthermore, their educational standard is low and their parents tend not to seek a discussion with the teacher. To a lesser extent this situation is also to be seen amongst semiskilled working-class families. Yet there is no evidence to suggest that parents in these social groups have any less concern for their children's welfare. The answer must surely be that either the statutory services are not in general seen by these parents as being relevant to their children's welfare; or else there are barriers, physical or psychological, to their attending. Certainly, the mothers more often go out to work; and they have more children in the family to care for. The services may not always be well sited for them.

To what extent does the inevitable social distance between these families and the staff of the services act as a deterrent? It is not necessary to assume that the families are regarded as inferior or even that they feel this to be the case; rather that the attitudes, values and standards which such families tend to find amongst those who staff the services may sometimes differ in important respects so that a common basis for effective communication is difficult. Whatever the reasons, it is important that these should be uncovered and understood and that services should seek, where necessary, to adapt in order to meet the needs of all their 'clients'.

Finally, what of the future of the study? In 1969 a second follow-up of the children was commenced. Broadly speaking, the same kind of information was collected and in the same way. Co-operation was once more forthcoming from every local authority in Britain and the parents and children, too, have been generous of their time in supporting the study. Information will be available on approximately 90 per cent of the children in the sample.

A number of general problems have begun to emerge which are related to the longitudinal nature of the project. The structure of the British educational system virtually imposes a four-yearly cycle on the collection of this type of information, i.e. at seven years, eleven years and at fifteen or sixteen years. These ages mark the end of infant schooling, junior schooling and secondary schooling for most of the children. However, if material for a new follow-up is to be sent out four years after the preceding one, work on the new follow-up (tracing the children, designing the interview schedules, etc.) must commence not later than three years after the preceding one. The completion, collection, checking and processing of the material for any follow-up takes approximately two years. This means that there is only time for one year's analysis before work on a new follow-up starts, which is insufficient for adequate exploitation of the material. The problem could in theory be solved by 'overlapping' research teams but it is inefficient for a new team to embark on a follow-up without drawing on the experience of the old team.

There is a further problem inherent in this situation. The local authorities and the many fieldworkers involved as well as the parents and children may be asked to co-operate in a new follow-up before they have had much feedback of results from the previous one.

The question of the nature of any feedback is also a difficult one to resolve. Information about the results is needed at different levels for different people. Parents are perhaps the single most difficult group to cater for in this respect. Some would no doubt appreciate detailed expositions, whilst others would be content to see occasional references in newspapers, which indicate that something of value has emerged as a result of their efforts.

Compromises have sometimes to be reached on these problems and it is often tempting to wish that the children could be held temporarily in a state of suspended animation whilst ideal solutions are reached!

Nevertheless, it is hoped that the results presented in this book and elsewhere will prove to be of value and of interest not only to those whose support and value have been so generously given but also to the much wider circle of people who are professionally concerned with children's health, education and welfare and, of course, to parents everywhere.

References

DOUGLAS, J. W. B. (1970) M.R.C. Unit, London School of Economics and Political Science, unpublished communication.
PRINGLE, M. L. KELLMER (1969) 'Policy implications of child development studies', *Concern*, no. 3. National Children's Bureau.
WISEMAN, S. (1970) The educational obstacle race: factors that hinder pupil progress. Director's address to the Annual Conference. National Foundation for Educational Research.

Subject Index